hattitude

D0690846

hattitude
knits for every mood

CATHY CARRON

sixth&spring books

sixth&spring books

233 Spring Street, New York, NY 10013

Managing Editor
WENDY WILLIAMS

Senior Editor
MICHELLE BREDESON

Art Director
DIANE LAMPHRON

Instructions Editor
PAT HARSTE

Technical Editors
CARLA SCOTT
ROSEMARY DRYSDALE
LORI STEINBERG

Yarn Editor
TANIS GRAY

Photography
ROSE CALLAHAN

Stylist
JULIE HINES

Hair and Makeup
INGEBORG K.

Vice President, Publisher
TRISHA MALCOLM

Creative Director
JOE VIOR

Production Manager
DAVID JOINNIDES

President
ART JOINNIDES

Copyright © 2009 by Cathy Carron
All rights reserved. No part of this publication may
be reproduced or used in any form or by any means—
graphic, electronic, or mechanical, including
photocopying, recording, or information storage-
and-retrieval systems—without written permission of
the publisher.

The written instructions, photographs, designs,
projects and patterns are intended for the personal,
noncommercial use of the retail purchaser and are
under federal copyright laws; they are not to be
reproduced in any form for commercial use. Permission
is granted to photocopy patterns for the personal use of
the retail purchaser.

Library of Congress Control Number: 2009928298
ISBN: 978-1-933027-85-2
Manufactured in China

1 3 5 7 9 10 8 6 4 2

First Edition

Acknowledgments

Third time around is the charm. And for this I have Trisha Malcolm to thank. She readily took me up on my book proposal and patiently saw me through the publishing process at Sixth&Spring Books. Her quiet but knowing demeanor was more than comforting. Many, many thanks.

Moreover, Trish's incredibly cohesive and competent staff was a pleasure to work with; this is a team that hums along with diligence and precision. I am indebted to my editor Michelle Bredeson for her calm patience and guidance; to Joe Vior for his keen art direction, color sense and sense of humor; to Tanis Gray for her vast knowledge of the yarn market and fab taste in all things knitted; to Julie Hines for her clever styling and to Pat Harste for carefully parsing and deciphering my written patterns. To all, I extend my thanks—it was a pleasure.

Much love and many thanks also go to my muse, Lydia, my youngest daughter, who inspires me and models for me. Her taste in all things fashion-related is quite wonderful; it's a joy to see it evolve and to learn from her as well. And, finally, to Andrew, my husband, my in-house tech guy and all-around Mr. Wonderful, many heartfelt thanks.

contents

idealistic my

prehensive oetic s

illing h

joyful ughtt

eas ergeti

schiev

aceful

kicky

Introduction

I'm in the mood...to knit some hats!

There's an old expression that says "clothes make the man." You could also say that the hat makes the woman, and the woman makes the hat! Once you've decided to knit a hat, you have to figure out what sort of hat to make. The choices are varied and vast. First, there's the general shape, then the color and texture and, finally, the detailing. What's a girl to do?

One way to decide is intuitively. How does a particular hat make you feel when you look at it? For some, getting dressed in the morning is a no-brainer—just slip on a carbon copy of what was worn the day before. Uniforms suit this type of person perfectly. However, many of us, the touchy-feely types, are ruled by our senses and momentary impulses. There are days I just couldn't bear to wear anything bright-colored, and yet on other days that screaming pink blouse beckons. Although they might not admit it, some guys even ponder their morning shirt and tie choices. I don't explicitly think about the "whys," but I do know my decisions are based on my mood when I roll out of bed in the morning. And what's wrong with that when the choice is there to be had?

When it comes to hand-knitting hats, the options expand even further with the plethora of yarn colors and textures available today; it's a veritable cornucopia. So take a look within, see how you respond to the each of the 40 designs, then cast on. And of course, you can always knit a different hat to suit every mood!

Never give up, and keep your ears warm.—Cathy

MATERIALS

Yarn
Montera **by Classic Elite Yarns, 3½oz/100g hanks, each approx 127yd/116m (llama/wool)**
- **1 hank each in #3887 pear (MC) and #3846 maquito teal (CC)**

Needles
- Size 9 (5.5mm) circular needles, 16"/40cm and 24"/60cm long or size to obtain gauge
- One set (4) size 9 (5.5mm) double-pointed needles (dpns)

Notions
- Stitch marker

ASYMMETRICAL BERET

This dramatic beret frames the face beautifully. Formed from the top down, its extra-wide brim is worked just like a traditional beret shape but is extended a bit longer. A contrasting stripe at the brow line makes it even more distinctive.

SIZES
Medium (Large)

FINISHED MEASUREMENTS
Circumference 18 (19⅓)"/45.5 (49.5)cm

GAUGE
16 sts and 24 rnds to 4"/10cm over St st using size 9 (5.5mm) circular needle.
Take time to check gauge.

STITCH GLOSSARY
inc Knit into front and back of stitch.

HAT
Crown
With dpn and MC, cast on 12 sts, leaving a long tail for sewing. Divide sts over 3 needles. Join and pm, taking care not to twist sts on needles.
Rnd 1 and all odd rnds Knit.
Rnd 2 *K1, inc 1 in next st; rep from * around—18 sts.
Rnd 4 *K2, inc 1 in next st; rep from * around—24 sts.
Rnd 6 *K3, inc 1 in next st; rep from * around—30 sts.
Rnd 8 *K4, inc 1 in next st; rep from * around—36 sts.
Rnd 10 *K5, inc 1 in next st; rep from * around—42 sts.
Rnd 12 *K6, inc 1 in next st; rep from * around—48 sts.
Rnd 14 *K7, inc 1 in next st; rep from * around—54 sts.
Rnd 16 *K8, inc 1 in next st; rep from * around—60 sts. Change to shorter circular needle. Cont to work one more k st before inc every other rnd 8 (9) times more, changing to longer circular needle—108 (114) sts.
Turn-of-crown
Purl next 2 rnds.
Rise
Knit next 2 rnds.
Rnd 1 *K16 (17), k2tog; rep from * around—102 (108) sts.
Rnd 2 and all even rnds Knit.
Rnd 3 *K15 (16), k2tog; rep from * around—96 (102) sts.
Rnd 5 *K14 (15), k2tog; rep from * around—90 (96) sts. Change to shorter circular needle. Cont to work one fewer k st before dec every other rnd 3 times more—72 (78) sts. Knit next rnd.
Band
Rnds 1 and 2 *K1, p1; rep from * around.
Rnds 3 and 4 With CC, rep rnds 1 and 2.
Rnds 5 and 6 With MC, rep rnds 1 and 2. Bind off loosely in rib.

FINISHING
Thread beg tail into tapestry needle. Weave tail around opening at top of crown. Pull tog tightly and secure end.❖

theatrical

MATERIALS

Yarn

Soft Chunky **by Twinkle by Wenlan/Classic Elite Yarns, 7oz/200g hank, approx 83yd/76m (wool)**
• 1 hank in #1 eggplant

Needles
• **Size 15 (10mm) circular needle, 16"/40cm long** or size to obtain gauge
• **One set (4) size 15 (10mm) double-pointed needles (dpns)**
• **Cable needle (cn)**

Notions
• **Stitch marker**

CHUNKY CABLED TOQUE

Everything about this sumptuous hat is generous—the extra-large cables that form a slight brim, the lush chunky yarn, and the deep purple hue, which is the color of royalty and riches. You'll probably want to keep it for yourself, though.

SIZE
One size fits all.

FINISHED MEASUREMENTS
Circumference 18"/45.5cm

GAUGE
8 sts and 10 rnds to 4"/10cm over St st using size 15 (10mm) circular needle. **Take time to check gauge.**

STITCH GLOSSARY
10-st RC Sl next 5 sts to cn and hold in back, k5, k5 from cn.
10-st LC Sl next 5 sts to cn and hold in front, k5, k5 from cn.
6-st RC Sl next 3 sts to cn and hold in back, k3, k3 from cn.
6-st LC Sl next 3 sts to cn and hold in front, k3, k3 from cn.

HAT

With circular needle, cast on 44 sts. Join, taking care not to twist sts on needle, pm for beg of rnds.
Rnds 1–6 K9, p3, k20, p3, k9.
Rnd 7 K9, p3, 10-st RC, 10-st LC, p3, k9.
Rnds 8–11 Rep rnd 1.
Rnds 12–21 Rep rnds 1–10.
Rnd 22 K7, k2tog tbl, p3, [k3, k2tog tbl] twice, [k2tog tbl, k3] twice, p3, k2tog tbl, k7—38 sts.
Rnds 23 and 24 Knit the k sts and purl the p sts.
Rnd 25 K6, k2tog tbl, p3, k2, [k2tog tbl] twice, k4, [k2tog tbl] twice, k2, p3, k2tog tbl, k6—32 sts.
Rnd 26 K7, p3, 6-st RC, 6-st LC, p3, k7.
Rnd 27 K5, k2tog tbl, p1, p2tog, k12, p2tog, p1, k2tog tbl, k5—28 sts.
Rnd 28 Knit the k sts and purl the p sts.
Rnd 29 K6, p2tog, k12, p2tog, k6—26 sts.
Rnd 30 Rep rnd 26.
Rnd 31 [K2tog tbl] 13 times—13 sts. Cut yarn leaving a 6"/15.5cm tail. Thread tail into tapestry needle, then thread through rem sts. Pull tog tightly and secure end. ❖

giving

MATERIALS

Yarn
Peruvia **by Berroco, Inc.,**
3½oz/100g hanks, each
approx 174yd/160m
(Peruvian highland wool)
• **1 hank in #7110 naranja**

Needles
• **Size 10 (6mm) circular**
needle, 16"/40cm long
or size to obtain gauge
• **One set (4) size 10 (6mm)**
double-pointed needles
(dpns)

Notions
• **Stitch marker**

BASKETWEAVE CAP

This basketweave pattern couldn't be simpler. It's easy to memorize and can even be "worked visually." The warm orange color and fun shape exude energy.

SIZES

Medium (Large)

FINISHED MEASUREMENTS

Circumference 19 (21)"/48 (53.5)cm

GAUGE

15 sts and 20 rnds to 4"/10cm over basketweave pat using size 10 (6mm) circular needle. **Take time to check gauge.**

NOTE

The hat is self-lined. After making the crown, you will cont with the inside rise, then the outside rise which gets folded over to the RS and stitched in place.

STITCH GLOSSARY

inc Knit into front and back of stitch.

BASKETWEAVE PATTERN

(multiple of 6 sts)
Rnds 1–4 *K1, p4, k1; rep from * around.
Rnd 5 Knit.
Rnds 6–9 *P2, k2, p2; rep from * around.
Rnd 10 Knit.
Rep rnds 1–10 for basketweave pat ITR.

HAT

Crown
With dpn, cast on 12 sts, leaving a long tail for sewing. Divide sts over 3 needles. Join, taking care not to twist sts on needles, pm for beg of rnds.
Rnd 1 Knit.

Rnd 2 [Inc in next st] 12 times—24 sts.
Rnds 3–5 Knit.
Rnd 6 *K1, inc in next st; rep from * around—36 sts.
Rnds 7–9 Knit.
Rnd 10 *K2, inc in next st; rep from * around—48 sts.
Rnds 11–13 Knit.
Rnd 14 *K3, inc in next st; rep from * around—60 sts.
Rnds 15–17 Knit.
Rnd 18 *K4, inc in next st; rep from * around—72 sts.
Rnds 19–21 Knit.
For Medium size only
Rnd 22 *K11, inc in next st; rep from * around—78 sts.
Rnds 23–24 Knit.
For both sizes
Change to circular needle. Purl next 2 rnds for turning ridge.
Inside rise
Work in St st for 5½"/14cm.
Outside rise
Turn crown and lining WS (purl side) out. Knit next 2 rnds. Rep rnds 1–10 of basketweave pat twice, then rnds 1–5 once. Bind off loosely knitwise; cut yarn, leaving a 24"/61cm tail.

FINISHING

Turn crown and lining RS (knit side) out. Thread beg tail into tapestry needle. Weave tail around opening at top of crown. Pull tog tightly and secure end. Fold basketweave pat side over to RS, so bound-off edge is even with turning ridge between crown and lining. Using ending tail, sew bound-off edge in place with a line of chain stitches (see page 96). ❖

vivacious

MATERIALS

Yarn
Bulky **by Blue Sky Alpacas**, 3½oz/100g hanks, each approx 45yd/41m (alpaca/wool)
• 1 hank each in #1009 bobcat (A), #1008 black bear (B) and #1007 gray wolf (C)

Needles
• Size 10½ (6.5mm) circular needle, 16"/40cm long
or size to obtain gauge
• One set (4) size 10½ (6.5mm) double-pointed needles (dpns)

Notions
• Stitch marker

TWO-TONED WATCH CAP

There's a lot to be said for a basic, cozy knitted cap. This one is knit in neutral colors in a fairly heavy gauge, and the increases from the top are distributed in a triangular fashion—a twist from the usual crown shape. Two-color blocking gives the illusion of a brim, but it would be equally cute in a solid color.

SIZES
Medium (Large)

FINISHED MEASUREMENTS
Circumference 19½ (22)"/49.5 (56)cm

GAUGES
15 sts and 13 rnds to 4"/10cm over k1, p1 rib using size 10½ (6.5mm) circular needle (unstretched).
11 sts and 13 rnds to 4"/10cm over k1, p1 rib using size 10½ (6.5mm) circular needle (slightly stretched).
Take time to check gauges.

HAT
Crown
With dpn and A, cast on 12 sts, leaving a long tail for sewing. Divide sts over 3 needles. Join, taking care not to twist sts on needles, pm for beg of rnds.
Rnd 1 Knit.
Rnd 2 *K1, m1, k1, p1, k1, m1; rep from * around twice more—18 sts.
Rnd 3 *K1, p1; rep from * around.
Rnd 4 *K1, m1, [p1, k1] twice, p1, m1; rep from * around twice more—24 sts.
Rnd 5 *K1, [k1, p1] 3 times, k1; rep from * around twice more.
Rnd 6 *K1, m1, [k1, p1] 3 times, k1, m1; rep from * around twice more—30 sts.
Rnd 7 *K1, p1; rep from * around.
Rnd 8 *K1, m1, [p1, k1] 4 times, p1, m1; rep from * around twice more—36 sts.
Rnd 9 *K1, [k1, p1] 5 times, k1; rep from * around twice more.
Rnd 10 *K1, m1, [k1, p1] 5 times, k1, m1; rep from * around twice more—42 sts.
Rnd 11 *K1, p1; rep from * around.
Rnd 12 *K1, m1, [p1, k1] 6 times, p1, m1; rep from * around twice more—48 sts.
Rnd 13 *K1, [k1, p1] 7 times, k1; rep from * around twice more.
Rnd 14 *K1, m1, [k1, p1] 8 times, k1, m1; rep from * around twice more—54 sts.
For Large size only
Rnd 15 *K1, p1; rep from * around.
Rnd 16 *K1, m1, [p1, k1] 8 times, p1, m1; rep from * around twice more—60 sts.
For both sizes
Change to circular needle.
Rise
Cont in rib as established until piece measures 6"/15cm from top of crown. Change to B. Work in rib for 3 (3½)"/7.5 (9)cm. Change to C. Bind off loosely in rib.

FINISHING
Thread beg tail into tapestry needle. Weave tail around opening at top of crown. Pull tog tightly and secure end. ❖

natural

MATERIALS

Yarn
Pure Wool DK **by Rowan/Westminster Fibers, Inc.,** 1¾oz/50g balls, each approx 137yd/125m (superwash wool)
- 3 balls in #28 raspberry

Needles
- **Size 6 (4mm) circular needle, 16"/40cm long** or size to obtain gauge
- **One set (4) size 6 (4mm) double-pointed needles (dpns)**

Notions
- **Stitch markers**
- **3"/76mm round acrylic buckle**

BUCKLED CLOCHE

Who could blame you for acting aloof in this chic cap? Its asymmetry starts subtly at the ribbed brim; after the brim, a portion of the ribbing is carried up through the hat's side to the top, where it becomes part of the side sash, a length of which is ribbed, then ruffled. A vintage buckle anchors it to the hat's side. Cool, collected style!

SIZES
Medium (Large)

FINISHED MEASUREMENTS
Circumference 19 (20½)"/48 (52)cm

GAUGE
24 sts and 28 rnds to 4"/10cm over St st using size 6 (4mm) circular needle.
Take time to check gauge.

STITCH GLOSSARY
inc Knit into front and back of stitch.

TWISTED RIB
(multiple of 2 sts)
Rnd 1 *K1 tbl, p1; rep from * around.
Rep rnd 1 for twisted rib.

HAT
Brim
With circular needle, cast on 114 (122) sts. Join, taking care not to twist sts on needle, pm for beg of rnds. Work around in twisted rib for 10 rnds.
Rise
Next rnd Work in twisted rib across first 30 sts, pm, k to end. Cont to work first 30 sts in twisted rib and rem 84 (92) sts in St st until piece measures 6 (6½)"/15.5 (16.5)cm from beg.

Crown
Rnd 1 Work in twisted rib to first marker, *k2tog; rep from * to end—72 (76) sts.
Rnd 2 Work in twisted rib to first marker, k to end.
Rnd 3 Work in twisted rib to first marker, k1, k2tog, k to last 2 sts, SKP—70 (74) sts.
Rnds 4–11 Rep rnds 2 and 3 4 times—62 (66) sts. Change to dpns.
Rnd 12 Work in twisted rib to first marker, [k2tog] 16 (18) times—46 (48) sts.
Rnd 13 Work in twisted rib to first marker, k to end.
Rnd 14 Work in twisted rib to first marker, [k2tog] 8 (9) times—38 (39) sts.
For Large size only
Next rnd Work in twisted rib to first marker, k3, k2tog, k4—38 sts.
For both sizes
Work even in pat sts on 38 sts as established for 7"/18cm.
Ruffle
Next rnd *Inc in next st, p1; rep from * around—57 sts.
Next rnd *K2, p1; rep from * around.
Next rnd *[Inc in next st] twice, p1; rep from * around—95 sts.
Next rnd *K4, p1; rep from * around.
Bind off in rib.

FINISHING
Position buckle in center of St st section, so crossbar of buckle is horizontal and bottom edge of buckle is 1¾"/4.5cm from bottom edge of hat. Sew crossbar in place. Fold top of hat over, then thread through buckle. ✤

haughty

MATERIALS

Yarn
Cashsoft Aran **by Rowan/Westminster Fibers, Inc.,** **1¾oz/50g balls, each approx 95yd/87m (extrafine merino/acrylic microfiber/cashmere)**
- **3 balls in #18 forest**

Needles
- **Size 8 (5mm) circular needles, 16"/40cm and 24"/61cm long**
or size to obtain gauge
- **One set (4) size 8 (5mm) double-pointed needles (dpns)**

Notions
- **Stitch holders**
- **Stitch marker**

TIED BONNET

The pioneer spirit lives on in this modest bonnet. Demure and traditional, it's a great shape to pair with a more modern coat. Willa Cather would be proud.

SIZES
Medium (Large)

FINISHED MEASUREMENTS
Circumference 18½ (21½)"/47 (54.5)cm

GAUGE
18 sts and 24 rnds to 4"/10cm over garter ridge st using size 8 (5mm) circular needle. **Take time to check gauge.**

STITCH GLOSSARY
inc Knit into front and back of stitch.

GARTER RIDGE STITCH
Rnds 1–3 Knit.
Rnd 4 Purl.
Rep rnds 1–4 for garter ridge st.

HAT
Crown
With dpn, cast on 12 sts, leaving a long tail for sewing. Divide sts over 3 needles. Join, taking care not to twist sts on needles, pm for beg of rnds.
Rnds 1, 3 and 5 Knit.
Rnd 2 [Inc in next st] 12 times—24 sts.
Rnd 4 Purl.
Rnd 6 *K1, inc in next st; rep from * around—36 sts.
Rnds 7–9 Rep rnds 3–5.
Rnd 10 *K2, inc in next st; rep from * around—48 sts.
Rnds 11–13 Rep rnds 3–5.
Rnd 14 *K3, inc in next st; rep from * around—60 sts.
Rnds 15–17 Rep rnds 3–5.
Rnd 18 *K4, inc in next st; rep from * around—72 sts.
Rnds 19–21 Rep rnds 3–5. Change to shorter circular needle.
Rnd 22 *K5, inc in next st; rep from * around—84 sts.
Rnds 23–25 Rep rnds 3–5.
Rnd 26 *K6, inc in next st; rep from * around—96 sts.
Rnds 27–29 Rep rnds 3–5.
Rnd 30 *K7, inc in next st; rep from * around—108 sts.
Rnds 31–33 Rep rnds 3–5.
Rnd 34 *K8, inc in next st; rep from * around—120 sts.
Rnds 37–39 Rep rnds 3–5.
Rnd 40 *K9, inc in next st; rep from * around—132 sts. Change to longer circular needle.
Rnds 41–43 Rep rnds 3–5.
For Large size only
Rnd 44 *K10, inc in next st; rep from * around—144 sts.
Rnds 45–47 Rep rnds 3–5.
For both sizes
Turn-of-crown
Rnd 1 *K9 (10), k2tog; rep from * around—120 (132) sts.
Rnd 2 Knit.
Rnd 3 Purl.
Rnd 4 *K8 (9), k2tog; rep from * around—108 (120) sts.
Rnd 5 Knit.
Rnd 6 Purl.
Rnd 7 *K7 (8), k2tog; rep from * around—96 (108) sts.
Rnd 8 Knit.
Rnd 9 Purl. Change to shorter circular needle.
Rnd 7 *K6 (7), k2tog; rep from * around—84 (96) sts.
Rnd 8 Knit.
Rnd 9 Purl. (Continued on page 90.)

humble

MATERIALS

Yarn
Angora Schulana **by Schulana/Skacel Collection, Inc.,** .4oz/10g balls, each approx 27yd/25m (angora)
• **4 balls in #310 olive/purple multi**

Needles
• **Size 7 (4.5mm) circular needle, 16"/40cm long** or size to obtain gauge
• **One set (4) size 7 (4.5mm) double-pointed needles (dpns)**

Notions
• **Stitch marker**

ANGORA CAP

Angora is one of the softest fibers around. It's also extremely lightweight and retains lots of heat. Here it's knit into the simplest of caps, ideal for popping in your pocket when not in use or slipping on when you want to go incognito.

SIZES
Medium (Large)

FINISHED MEASUREMENTS
Circumference 19 (20½)"/48 (52)cm

GAUGE
16 sts and 22 rnds to 4"/10cm over St st using size 7 (4.5mm) circular needle.
Take time to check gauge.

STITCH GLOSSARY
inc Knit into front and back of stitch.

HAT
Crown
With dpn, cast on 12 sts, leaving a long tail for sewing. Divide sts over 3 needles. Join, taking care not to twist sts on needles, pm for beg of rnds.
Rnd 1 and all odd rnds Knit.
Rnd 2 *K1, inc in next st; rep from * around—18 sts.
Rnd 4 *K2, inc in next st; rep from * around—24 sts.
Rnd 6 *K3, inc in next st; rep from * around—30 sts.
Rnd 8 *K4, inc in next st; rep from * around—36 sts.
Rnd 10 *K5, inc in next st; rep from * around—42 sts.
Rnd 12 *K6, inc in next st; rep from * around—48 sts.
Rnd 14 *K7, inc in next st; rep from * around—54 sts.
Rnd 16 *K8, inc in next st; rep from * around—60 sts. Cont to work one more k st before inc every other rnd 6 (7) times more, changing to circular needle when there are too many sts to work comfortably on dpns—96 (102) sts. Knit next 3 rnds.
Rise shaping
Rnd (dec) 1 *K22 (23), k2tog, k22 (24) k2tog; rep from * around once more—92 (98) sts.
Rnds 2 and 3 Knit.
Rnd (dec) 4 *K21 (22), k2tog, k21 (23) k2tog; rep from * around once more—88 (94) sts.
Rnds 5 and 6 Knit.
Rnd (dec) 7 *K20 (21), k2tog, k20 (22) k2tog; rep from * around once more—84 (90) sts.
Rnds 8 and 9 Knit.
Rnd (dec) 10 *K19 (20), k2tog, k19 (21) k2tog; rep from * around once more—80 (86) sts.
Rnds 11 and 12 Knit.
Rnd (dec) 13 *K18 (19), k2tog, k18 (20) k2tog; rep from * around once more—76 (82) sts.
Rnds 14–23 Knit.
I-cord edging
Cast on 3 sts to LH needle.
Next rnd *K2, k2tog tbl, slip the 3 sts on RH needle back to LH needle; rep from * around. Bind off last 3 sts knitwise. Cut yarn, leaving a long tail for sewing.

FINISHING
Thread beg tail into tapestry needle. Weave tail around opening at top of crown. Pull tog tightly to close opening; secure end. Sew ends of I-cord edging together. ❧

mysterious

MATERIALS

Yarn
Chenille Thick & Quick **by Lion Brand Yarn, 3½oz/100g skeins, each approx 100yd/90m (acrylic/rayon)**
- **1 skein each in #99 chardonnay (A) and #107 periwinkle (B)**

Needles
- **Size 11 (8mm) circular needle, 16"/40cm long** or size to obtain gauge
- **One set (4) size 11 (8mm) double-pointed needles (dpns)**

Notions
- **Stitch marker**

STRIPED SHERPA HAT

A new, noble and nifty take on chunky chenille fiber. The chenille gives the hat enough structure to stand on its own, but it can also be shaped to fall however you want. The striping gives it an exotic feel, either medieval Venice or current-day Mali—you choose. Two colors of yarn are used with one carried behind the other—just remember to keep the tension, even when switching colors.

SIZES
Medium (Large)

FINISHED MEASUREMENTS
Circumference 20 (22)"/51 (56)cm

GAUGE
12 sts and 16 rnds to 4"/10cm over stripe pat using size 11 (8mm) circular needle. **Take time to check gauge.**

NOTES
1) When changing colors, pick up new color from under dropped color to prevent holes.
2) Carry color not in use loosely across WS of work.

STRIPE PATTERN (multiple of 2 sts)
Rnd 1 *K1, with A, k1 with B; rep from * around.
Rep rnd 1 for stripe pat.

HAT
Rise
With circular needle, cast on as foll: *Cast on 1 with A, cast on 1 with B; rep from * until there are 60 (66) sts on needle. Join, taking care not to twist sts on needle, pm for beg of rnds. Cont in stripe pat until piece measures 8"/20.5cm from beg.

Crown
Dec rnd 1 *With A, k2tog, with B, k2tog, work in stripe pat over next 16 (18) sts; rep from * around twice more—54 (60) sts. Work next rnd even in stripe pat.

Dec rnd 2 *With A, k2tog, with B, k2tog, work in stripe pat over next 14 (16) sts; rep from * around twice more—48 (54) sts. Work next rnd even in stripe pat.

Dec rnd 3 *With A, k2tog, with B, k2tog, work in stripe pat over next 12 (14) sts; rep from * around twice more—42 (48) sts. Work next rnd even in stripe pat. Change to dpns.

Dec rnd 4 *With A, k2tog, with B, k2tog, work in stripe pat over next 10 (12) sts; rep from * around twice more—36 (42) sts. Work next rnd even in stripe pat.

Dec rnd 5 *With A, k2tog, with B, k2tog; rep from * around—18 (21) sts. Cut B.

Dec rnd 6 With A [k2tog] 9 (10) times, k0 (1)—9 (11) sts. Cut yarn leaving a 8"/20.5cm tail. Thread tail in tapestry needle, then thread through rem sts. Pull tog tightly and secure end. ❖

dignified

MATERIALS

Yarn

Burley Spun **by Brown Sheep Company**, 8oz/226g hanks, each approx 130yd/119m (wool)
- **1 hank each in #BS38 lotus pink (MC) and #BS39 periwinkle (A)**

Lamb's Pride Bulky **by Brown Sheep Company**, 4oz/113g skeins, each approx 125yd/114m (wool/mohair)
- **1 skein each in #M102 orchid thistle (B) and #M83 raspberry (D)**

La Gran **by Classic Elite Yarns**, 1⅛oz/42g ball, approx 90yd/82m (mohair/wool/nylon)
- **1 ball in #61556 lovely lilac (C)**

Needles
- **Two size 11 (8mm) circular needles, 16"/40cm long**
  or size to obtain gauge
- **One set (4) size 11 (8mm) double-pointed needles (dpns)**

Notions
- **Stitch holders**
- **Stitch marker**
- **Pencil compass**

EARMUFF HAT

Although this flapped hat is Nordic in inspiration, it is no doubt channeling a certain *Star Wars* princess as well. The felted flowers (great use of scrap yarn) are attached with French knots in a snappy contrasting color.

SIZES
Medium (Large)

FINISHED MEASUREMENTS
Circumference 19 (21½)"/48 (54.5)cm

GAUGE
10 sts and 20 rnds to 4"/10cm over St st using size 11 (8mm) circular needle and MC.
Take time to check gauge.

STITCH GLOSSARY
inc Knit into front and back of stitch.

SEED STITCH
(multiple of 2 sts)
Rnd 1 *K1, p1; rep from * around.
Rnd 2 Knit the p sts and purl the k sts.
Rep rnd 2 for seed st ITR.

GARTER STITCH
Rnd 1 Knit.
Rnd 2 Purl.
Rep rnds 1 and 2 for garter st ITR.

HAT
Crown
With dpn and MC, cast on 12 sts, leaving a long tail for sewing. Divide sts over 3 needles. Join, taking care not to twist sts on needles, pm for beg of rnds.
Rnd 1 and all odd rnds Knit.
Rnd 2 *K1, inc in next st; rep from * around—18 sts.
Rnd 4 *K2, inc in next st; rep from * around—24 sts.
Rnd 6 *K3, inc in next st; rep from * around—30 sts.
Rnd 8 *K4, inc in next st; rep from * around—36 sts. Cont to work one more k st before inc every other rnd 2 (3) times more—48 (54) sts. Change to circular needle. Knit next rnd.
Rise
Cont to work even in seed st until piece measures 7"/17.5cm from top of crown.
Brim
Change to A. Cont in garter st for 6 rnds.
Next rnd Bind off 6 sts, k11 (13) sts, place 12 (14) sts on RH needle on a holder, bind off next 13 (15) sts, k11 (13) sts, place 12 (14) sts on RH needle on a holder, bind off rem sts.
Earflaps
Place 12 (14) sts from one holder onto a dpn. Join A. Working back and forth using 2 dpns, cont in garter st for 8 rows.
Next (dec) row K1, k2tog, k to last 3 sts, k2tog, k1. Rep last row twice times more. Bind off rem 6 (8) sts knitwise. Rep for second ear flap.

FLOWER APPLIQUÉS (make 2)
With circular needle and B and C held tog, cast on 20 sts. Work back and forth in St st for 6"/15cm. Bind off loosely knitwise.

FINISHING
Thread beg tail of hat into tapestry needle. Weave tail around opening at top of crown. Pull tog tightly and secure end.
Felting
Place flower appliqués in washing machine set to hot wash/cold rinse with (Continued on page 90.)

fanciful

MATERIALS

Yarn
Como **by Debbie Bliss/KFI**, 1¾oz/50g balls, each approx 46yd/42m (wool/cashmere)
• **4 balls in #7 denim**

Needles
• **Two size 10½ (6.5mm) circular needles, 16"/40cm long** or size to obtain gauge
• **One set (4) size 10½ (6.5mm) double-pointed needles (dpns)**

Notions
• **Stitch marker**

CHUNKY KNIT BUCKET HAT

This high topper brings to mind the turban of a medium or of the muse for a present-day Vermeer. It knits up quickly in the round from the top down and is then worked back and forth with added stitches for the band and "butterfly" detail. But you already knew that, didn't you?

SIZES
Medium (Large)

FINISHED MEASUREMENTS
Circumference 20 (23)"/51 (58.5)cm

GAUGE
12 sts and 18 rnds to 4"/10cm over garter ridge st using size 10½(6.5mm) circular needle.
Take time to check gauge.

STITCH GLOSSARY
inc Knit into front and back of stitch.

GARTER RIDGE STITCH
(multiple of 10 sts)
Rnd 1 *K4, p6; rep from * around.
Rnds 2–4 Knit.
Rnd 5 *P5, k4, p1; rep from * around.
Rnds 6–8 Knit.
Rep rnds 1–8 for garter ridge st.

HAT
Crown
With dpn, cast on 12 sts, leaving a long tail for sewing. Divide sts over 3 needles. Join, taking care not to twist sts on needles, pm for beg of rnds.

Rnds 1 and 2 Knit.
Rnd 3 [Inc in next st] 12 times—24 sts.
Rnds 4–6 Knit.
Rnd 7 [inc in next st] 24 times—48 sts.
Rnd 8–10 Knit.
Rnd 11 *K3, inc in next st; rep from * around—60 sts.
Rnds 12–14 Knit.
For Large size only
Rnd 15 *K5, inc in next st; rep from * around—70 sts.
Rnd 16 Knit.
For both sizes
Change to circular needle.
Rise
Rep rnds 1–8 of garter ridge st 5 times.
Brim
You will now be working back and forth using 2 circular needles.
Row 1 [K1, m1] twice, k to last 2 sts, [m1, k1] twice—64 (74) sts.
Row 2 Knit. Rep last 2 rows 5 times more. Bind off loosely knitwise.

FINISHING
Thread beg tail into tapestry needle. Weave tail around opening at top of crown. Pull tog tightly to close opening; secure end. Fold brim over to RS. At the bound-off edge of brim, hold the two shaped edges together at their bases, then tack together to secure. Fold the RH shaped edge in half to the right, then tack the point to the brim. Fold the LH shaped edge in half to the left, then tack the point to the brim. ❧

insightful

MATERIALS

Yarn
Chunky **by Misti Alpaca,**
3½oz/100g hanks,
each approx 108yd/98m
(baby alpaca)
• **2 hanks in #2L471 black/gray**
moulinette

Needles
• **Size 11 (8mm) circular**
needle, 16"/40cm long
or size to obtain gauge
• **One set (4) size 11 (8mm)**
double-pointed needles (dpns)

Notions
• **Stitch marker**
• **2¼yd/2m of red leather lacing**

TWEED CLOCHE

Travel back in time to the Roaring
Twenties in this retro-style cloche. You'll
be in style both in the country and out
on the town. The rawhide drawstring
adds just a touch of color.

SIZES

Medium (Large)

FINISHED MEASUREMENTS

Circumference 20 (22)"/51 (56)cm

GAUGE

12 sts and 16 rnds to 4"/10cm over St st
using size 11 (8mm) circular needle.
Take time to check gauge.

STITCH GLOSSARY

inc Knit into front and back of stitch.

HAT
Crown

With dpn, cast on 12 sts, leaving a long
tail for sewing. Divide sts over 3 needles.
Join, taking care not to twist sts on
needles, pm for beg of rnds.
Rnd 1 and all odd rnds Knit.
Rnd 2 *K1, inc in next st; rep from *
around—18 sts.
Rnd 4 *K2, inc in next st; rep from *
around—24 sts.
Rnd 6 *K3, inc in next st; rep from *
around—30 sts.
Rnd 8 *K4, inc in next st; rep from *
around—36 sts.
Rnd 10 *K5, inc in next st; rep from *
around—42 sts.
Rnd 12 *K6, inc in next st; rep from *
around—48 sts.
Rnd 14 *K7, inc in next st; rep from *
around—54 sts.
Rnd 16 *K8, inc in next st; rep from *
around—60 sts.
For Large size only
Rnd 17 Knit.
Rnd 18 *K9, inc in next st; rep from *
around—66 sts.
For both sizes
Change to circular needle.
Rise
Cont in St st until piece measures 7½
(8)"/19 (20.5)cm from top of crown.
Brim
Next (inc) rnd *K3, inc in next st; rep
from * around, end k0 (2)—75 (82) sts.
Knit next 8 rnds.
Next (eyelet) rnd *K2tog, yo; rep from *
around, end k1 (0). Knit next rnd.
Next (dec) rnd *K3, k2tog; rep from *
around, end k0 (2)—60 (66) sts. Bind off
loosely knitwise; cut yarn leaving a
24"/61cm tail.

FINISHING

Thread beg tail into tapestry needle.
Weave tail around opening at top of
crown. Pull tog tightly and secure end.
Fold brim 2½"/6.5cm over to RS. Using
ending tail, tack bound-off edge of brim
to sides of hat. Fold lacing in half
forming a loop. Beg at center of RH side
of hat, weave cut ends of lacing through
eyelets. To tie lacing, first insert ends
through loop, then pull on ends to adjust
hat to fit your head. Now, insert ends
under horizontal lacing to the right of
loop so they exit at top. Now bring cut
ends to the right, then under themselves
so they exit at bottom. Tighten knot,
then trim ends to desired length. ❖

nostalgic

MATERIALS

Yarn
Cashsoft Aran **by Rowan/Westminster Fibers, Inc.**, 1¾oz/50g balls, each approx 95yd/87m (extrafine merino/acrylic microfiber/cashmere)
• 4 balls in #1 oat

Needles
• **Size 6 (4mm) circular needle, 24"/61cm long** or size to obtain gauge
• **Cable needle (cn)**

CABLE-EDGED KERCHIEF

Calm your tresses and your mood with this simple kerchief. Although it's tempting to work this design up in a traditional lacy texture, here the body is knit in stockinette stitch and edged with a subtle half cable.

SIZE
One size fits all.

FINISHED MEASUREMENTS
Approx 20"/51cm wide x 14"/35.5cm long (excluding ties)

GAUGE
18 sts and 24 rows to 4"/10cm over St st using size 6 (4mm) circular needle.
Take time to check gauge.

STITCH GLOSSARY
inc Knit into front and back of stitch.
6-st LC Sl next 3 sts to cn and hold in front, k3, k3 from cn.

KERCHIEF
With circular needle, cast on 4 sts. Work back and forth as foll:
Row 1 (RS) Knit.
Row 2 and all WS rows Purl.
Row 3 K1, m1, k to last st, m1, k1—6 sts. Rep rows 2 and 3 until there are 90 sts on needle, end with a WS row.
Ties
Next row (RS) Knit across, casting on 60 sts at end of row—150 sts.
Next row Purl across, casting on 60 sts at end of row—210 sts. Work even in St st for 8 rows.

Front edging
Row 1 (RS) K1, *inc in next st; rep from * across, end k1—418 sts.
Row 2 Purl.
Row 3 Knit.
Row 4 Purl.
Row 5 K2, *6-st LC; rep from *, end k2 to end.
Row 6 Purl. Bind off all sts loosely knitwise.
Left side edging
With RS facing and circular needle, pick up and k 108 sts evenly spaced along left edge of kerchief from end of tie to center bottom point. Work back and forth as foll:
Row 1 (WS) Purl.
Row 2 K1, *inc in next st; rep from * across, end k1—214 sts.
Row 3 Purl.
Row 4 Knit.
Row 5 Purl.
Row 6 K2, *6-st LC; rep from *, end k2 to end.
Row 7 Purl. Bind off all sts loosely knitwise.
Right side edging
With RS facing and circular needle, pick up and k 108 sts evenly spaced along left edge of kerchief from center bottom point to end of tie. Cont to work same as left side edging.

FINISHING
Sew side edges of side edgings together at center bottom point. Block kerchief so edgings lie flat. ❖

peaceful

MATERIALS

Yarn
Lamb's Pride Bulky **by Brown Sheep Company, 4oz/113g skeins, each approx 125yd/114m (wool/mohair)**
• **1 skein each in #M05 onyx (A), #M10 creme (B), #M38 lotus pink (C) and #M110 orange you glad (D)**

Needles
• **Size 10½ (6.5mm) circular needle,** 16"/40cm long
or size to obtain gauge
• **One set (4) size 10¼ (6.5mm) double-pointed needles (dpns)**

Notions
• **Stitch marker**

BARGELLO-STITCH HAT

With its graphic pattern and bold colors, this hat is as eyecatching as your smile. Needlepoint enthusiasts will recognize the "bargello" stitch. Alternating colors are knit in a simple (only complicated-*looking*) pattern starting from the top downward. It's also a fun way to use up your stash yarns!

SIZES
Medium (Large)

FINISHED MEASUREMENTS
Circumference 20 (22½)"/51 (57)cm

GAUGE
12 sts and 14 rnds to 4"/10cm over St st using size 10½ (6.5mm) circular needle. Take time to check gauge.

STITCH GLOSSARY
inc Knit into front and back of stitch.

HAT
Crown
With dpn and A, cast on 12 sts, leaving a long tail for sewing. Divide sts over 3 needles. Join, taking care not to twist sts on needles, pm for beg of rnds.
Rnd 1 Knit.
Rnd 2 [Inc in next st] 12 times—24 sts.
Rnd 3 Knit.
Rnd 4 [Inc in next st] 24 times—48 sts.
Rnd 5 Knit.
Rnd 6 *K3, inc in next st; rep from * around—60 sts.
Rnd 7 Knit.
For Large size only
Rnd 8 *K6, inc in next st; rep from *
around, end k4—68 sts.
Rnd 9 Knit.
For both sizes
Change to circular needle.
Rise
With B, knit next 4 rnds.
Rnd 1 With C, *k3, insert RH needle in next st of 3 rnds below, yo and pull up a loop, k1, pass loop over last st knit; rep from * around.
Rnds 2–4 With C, knit.
Rnd 5 With A, *k1, insert RH needle in next st of 3 rnds below, yo and pull up a loop, k1, pass loop over last st knit, k2; rep from * around.
Rnds 6–8 With A, knit.
Rnds 9–12 With B, rep rnds 1–4.
Rnds 13–16 With D, rep rnds 5–8.
Rnds 17–20 With A, rep rnds 1–4.
Rnds 21–24 With B, rep rnds 5–8.
Rnds 25–28 With C, rep rnds 1–4.
Rnd 29 With A, rep rnd 1.
Brim
For Medium size only
Next (inc) rnd With A, *K5, inc in next st; rep from * around—70 sts.
For Large size only
Next (inc) rnd With A, *K6, inc in next st; rep from * around, end k4, inc in next st—78 sts.
For both sizes
With A, cont in k1, p1 rib for 4 rnds. Bind off loosely in rib.

FINISHING
Thread beg tail into tapestry needle. Weave tail around opening at top of crown. Pull tog tightly and secure end.✢

outgoing

MATERIALS

Yarn
Glitterspun **by Lion Brand Yarn**, 1¾oz/50g skeins, each approx 115yd/105m (acrylic/cupro/polyester)
• 2 skeins in #150 silver

Needles
• Size 10 (6mm) circular needle, 16"/40cm long
or size to obtain gauge

Notions
• Stitch marker
• 340 (360, 380) 7mm silver pony beads

BEADED FRINGE HAT

This impish number doubles as a neck gaiter. Knit in silver yarn and edged with metallic pony beads, it's a real dazzler. The ribbed structure couldn't be simpler, but stringing and attaching the beads does take some time.

SIZES
Medium (Large)

FINISHED MEASUREMENTS
Circumference 19½ (21½)"/49.5 (54.5)cm

GAUGE
14 sts and 22 rnds to 4"/10cm over k2, p2 rib using size 10 (6mm) circular needle and yarn held doubled (slightly stretched).
Take time to check gauge.

NOTES
Yarn is held double throughout.

HAT

With circular needle and 2 strands held tog, cast on 68 (76) sts. Join and pm taking care not to twist sts on needle. Work around in k2, p2 rib for 6"/15cm. Bind off loosely in rib.

BEADED FRINGE

Cut 34 (38) 12"/30.5cm strands of yarn. Thread a strand in tapestry needle. With RS of bound-off edge facing, insert needle between 2 knit (or purl) sts and draw yarn through; remove needle. Even up yarns ends, then tie in a firm square knot. Cont to work in this manner around. For each pair of strands, thread one end into tapestry needle, then thread on 5 pony beads; remove needle. Tie end into a triple knot to prevent beads from falling off. Rep for second strand. Cont to work in this manner around.❖

miSchievouS

MATERIALS

Yarn
2-Ply Mongolian Cashmere
**by Jade Sapphire Exotic Fibres,
2oz/55g hanks, each approx
400yd/366m**
- **1 hank in #88 verdigris**

Needles
- **Size 2 and 6 (2.75 and 4mm)
circular needles, 16"/40cm long**
or size to obtain gauge
- **One set (4) size 6 (4mm)
double-pointed needles (dpns)**

Notions
- **Stitch marker**

CASHMERE BERET

In this finely knit, featherweight beret, you'll look as cool and confident as blue cashmere. The super-wide, open twisted rib band fits snugly to contrast with the floppier seed stitch crown, giving it a rakish air.

SIZES
Medium (Large)

FINISHED MEASUREMENTS
Circumference 18½ (19¾)"/47 (50)cm

GAUGE
28 sts and 36 rnds to 4"/10cm over seed st using larger circular needle.
Take time to check gauge.

STITCH GLOSSARY
inc Knit into front and back of stitch.

OPEN TWISTED RIB
(multiple of 5 sts)
Rnd 1 *K2, p1, k1 tbl, p1; rep from * around.
Rnd 2 *K1, yo, k1, p1, k1 tbl, p1; rep from * around.
Rnd 3 *K3, p1, k1 tbl, p1; rep from * around.
Rnd 4 *K3, pass the first of these 3 sts on RH needle over the second 2 sts, p1, k1 tbl, p1; rep from * around.
Rep rnds 1–4 for open twisted rib.

SEED STITCH
(multiple of 2 sts)
Rnd 1 *K1, p1; rep from * around.
Rnd 2 Knit the p sts and purl the k sts.
Rep rnd 2 for seed st.

HAT
With smaller circular needle, cast on 135 (145) sts. Join, taking care not to twist sts on needle, pm for beg of rnds. Rep rnds 1–4 of open twisted rib 9 times.
Next (inc) rnd *K4, inc in next st; rep from * around—162 (174) sts. Change to larger circular needle. Cont in seed st for 6"/15cm.
Crown
Rnd 1 *K4, k2tog; rep from * around—135 (145) sts. Change to dpns.
Rnd 2 *K3, k2tog; rep from * around—108 (116) sts.
Rnd 3 *K2, k2tog; rep from * around—81 (87) sts.
Rnd 4 *K2tog; rep from * around, end k1—41 (44) sts.
Rnd 1 *K2tog; rep from * around, end k1 (0)—21 (22) sts. Cut yarn, leaving a 6"/15.5cm tail. Thread tail into tapestry needle, then thread through rem sts. Pull tog tightly and secure end. ❧

aloof

MATERIALS

Yarn

Sport Weight **by Blue Sky Alpacas, 1¾oz/50g hanks, each approx 110yd/100m (baby alpaca)**
- **1 hank each in #507 natural light gray (A), #508 natural medium gray (B) and #509 natural dark gray (C)**

Needles
- **Size 4 (3.5mm) circular needle, 16"/40cm long** or size to obtain gauge
- **One set (4) size 4 (3.5mm) double-pointed needles (dpns)**

Notions
- **Stitch marker**

STRIPED BEANIE

Just the facts, ma'am. Simple shape, super-soft alpaca yarn, skinny stripe pattern, allover textured surface. Very subtle, very chic. And the perfect hat for a girl who doesn't mess around.

SIZES

Medium (Large)

FINISHED MEASUREMENTS

Circumference 19¼(21)"/49 (53.5)cm

GAUGE

20 sts and 32 rnds to 4"/10cm over broken rib pat (slightly stretched) using size 4 (3.5mm) circular needle.
Take time to check gauge.

BROKEN RIB AND STRIPE PATTERN

(multiple of 4 sts)
Rnd 1 With A, knit.
Rnd 2 With A, *k2, p2; rep from * around.
Rnd 3 With B, knit.
Rnd 4 With B, *k2, p2; rep from * around.
Rnd 5 With C, knit.
Rnd 6 With C, *k2, p2; rep from * around.
Rep rnds 1–6 for broken rib and stripe pat.

HAT

With circular needle and A, cast on 96 (104) sts. Join, taking care not to twist sts on needles, pm for beg of rnds. Work in broken rib and stripe pat until piece measures 8"/20.5cm from beg.

Crown

Cont in stripe pat as established, work as foll:
Rnd 1 *K2tog; rep from * around—48 (52) sts.
Rnd 2 Knit.
Rnd 3 *K2tog; rep from * around—24 (26) sts.
Rnd 4 Knit.
Rnd 5 *K2tog; rep from * around—12 (13) sts.
Rnd 6 Knit. Cut yarn, leaving a 6"/15.5cm tail. Thread tail in tapestry needle, then thread through rem sts. Pull tog tightly and secure end. ❖

matter-of-fact

MATERIALS

Yarn
Angora Schulana **by Schulana/Skacel Collection, Inc., .4oz/10g balls, each approx 27yd/25m (angora)**
- 10 (12) balls in #93 orange

Needles
- **Size 7 (4.5mm) circular needle, 16"/40cm long** or size to obtain gauge
- **One set (4) size 7 (4.5mm) double-pointed needles (dpns)**

Notions
- **Stitch marker**

FLOPPY TOQUE

Cozy up with a good book in this oversized, vibrantly colored angora cap. Lusciously warm and luxurious, angora is the fashion equivalent of mac 'n cheese.

SIZES
Medium (Large)

FINISHED MEASUREMENTS
Circumference 19 (22)"/48 (56)cm

GAUGE
14 sts and 24 rnds to 4"/10cm over St st using size 7 (4.5mm) circular needle and yarn held doubled.
Take time to check gauge.

NOTE
Use 2 strands of yarn held tog throughout.

STITCH GLOSSARY
inc Knit into front and back of stitch.

HAT
Crown
With dpn and 2 strands of yarn held tog, cast on 12 sts, leaving a long tail for sewing. Divide sts over 3 needles. Join, taking care not to twist sts on needles, pm for beg of rnds.
Rnd 1 and all odd rnds Knit.
Rnd 2 *K1, inc in next st; rep from * around—18 sts.
Rnd 4 *K2, inc in next st; rep from * around—24 sts.
Rnd 6 *K3, inc in next st; rep from * around—30 sts.
Rnd 8 *K4, inc in next st; rep from * around—36 sts.
Rnd 10 *K5, inc in next st; rep from * around—42 sts. Cont to work one more k st before inc every other rnd 7(9) times more—84 (96) sts. Change to circular needle.
Rise shaping
Rnd 1 and all odd rnds Knit.
Rnd 2 *K12(14), k2tog; rep from * around—78 (90) sts.
Rnd 4 *K11(13), k2tog; rep from * around—72 (84) sts
Rnd 6 *K10(12), k2tog; rep from * around—66 (78) sts. Work even for 5½ (5)"/14 (12.5)cm.
Brim
Work in k1, p1 rib for 6"/15cm. Bind off in rib.

FINISHING
Thread beg tail into tapestry needle. Weave tail around opening at top of crown. Pull tog tightly to close opening; secure end. ♣

literary

MATERIALS

Yarn
Berkshire Bulky **by Valley Yarns**, 3½oz/100g skeins, each approx 108yd/99m (wool/alpaca)
• 1 skein each in #19 fuchsia (A), #22 amethyst (B) and #20 plum (C)

Needles
• Size 10½ (6.5mm) circular needle, 16"/40cm long or size to obtain gauge
• One set (4) size 10½ (6.5mm) double-pointed needles (dpns)

Notions
• Stitch markers

STRIPED EYELET CAP

This simple, lively topper is perfect for the gal on the go. It's worked in tonal, multi-colors from the top down in eyelet picot. The body of the hat is a modified beret shape, which ends with a kicky upturned, asymmetrical brim.

SIZE
One size fits all.

FINISHED MEASUREMENTS
Circumference 20"/51cm

GAUGE
12 sts and 20 rnds to 4"/10cm over eyelet pat using size 10½(6.5mm) circular needle.
Take time to check gauge.

STITCH GLOSSARY
inc Knit into front and back of stitch.

EYELET PATTERN
Rnds 1–3 Knit.
Rnd 4 Purl.
Rnd 5 *K2tog, yo; rep from * around.
Rnd 6 Purl.
Rep rnds 1–6 for eyelet pat.

HAT
Crown
With dpn and A, cast on 10 sts, leaving a long tail for sewing. Divide sts over 3 needles. Join taking care not to twist sts on needles, pm for beg of rnds.
Rnd 1 Knit.
Rnd 2 [Inc in next st] 10 times—20 sts.
Rnd 3 Knit. Change to B.
Rnd 4 Purl.
Rnd 5 *K2tog, yo; rep from * around.
Rnd 6 Purl. Change to A.
Rnd 7 Knit.
Rnd 8 *K1, inc in next st; rep from * around—30 sts.
Rnd 9 Knit. Change to C.

Rnds 10–12 Rep rnds 4–6. Change to A.
Rnd 13 Knit.
Rnd 14 *K2, inc in next st; rep from * around—40 sts.
Rnd 15 Knit. Change to B.
Rnds 16–18 Rep rnds 4–6. Change to A.
Rnd 19 Knit.
Rnd 20 *K3, inc in next st; rep from * around—50 sts. Change to circular needle.
Rnd 21 Knit. Change to C.
Rnds 22–24 Rep rnds 4–6. Change to A.
Rnd 25 Knit.
Rnd 26 *K4, inc in next st; rep from * around—60 sts.
Rnd 27 Knit. Change to B.
Rise
Rnds 28–30 Rep rnds 4–6. Change to A.
Rnd 31 Knit.
Rnd 32 *K5, inc in next st; rep from * around—70 sts.
Rnd 33 Knit. Change to C.
Rnds 34–36 Rep rnds 4–6. Change to A.
Rnd 37 Knit.
Rnd 38 *K6, inc in next st; rep from * around—80 sts.
Rnd 39 Knit. Change to B.
Rnds 40–42 Rep rnds 4–6. Change to A.
Rnds 43–45 Knit. Change to C.
Rnds 46–48 Rep rnds 4–6. Change to A.
Rnd 49 Knit.
Rnd 50 *K6, k2tog; rep from * around—70 sts.
Rnd 51 Knit. Change to B.
Rnds 52–54 Rep rnds 4–6. Change to A.
Rnd 55 Knit.
Rnd 56 *K5, k2tog; rep from * around—60 sts.
Rnd 57 Knit.
Brim
With A only, cont as foll:
Rnds 1 and 2 *K1, p1; rep from * around.
Rnd 3 Work in rib across 48 sts; turn, (Continued on page 90.)

energetic

MATERIALS

Yarn

Ultra Alpaca **by Berroco, Inc., 3½oz/100g hanks, each approx 215yd/198m (super fine alpaca/peruvian highland wool)**
- **1 hank each in #6257 chambray (A), #6233 rose spice (B), #6291 yucca mix (C), #6236 chianti (D), #6234 cardinal (E), #6240 blue violet (F) and #6294 turquoise mix (G)**

Needles
- **Two size 6 (4mm) circular needles, 16"/40cm long**
or size to obtain gauge
- **One set (4) size 6 (4mm) double-pointed needles (dpns)**

Notions
- **Stitch marker**

FAIR ISLE STOCKING CAP

Tons of color, a perky pompom and quirky flaps add up to a hat that's ready for action, whether you're skiing down the slopes or bopping around town. If you love color, Fair Isle is a knitting must. The harmonious patterns and variety of colors you can achieve are amazing.

SIZES
Medium (Large)

FINISHED MEASUREMENTS
Circumference 18 (19¼)"/45.5 (49)cm

GAUGES
23 sts and 26 rnds to 4"/10cm over St st and chart pats using size 6 (4mm) circular needle.
24 sts and 28 rnds to 4"/10cm over k2, p2 rib (slightly stretched) using size 6 (4mm) circular needle.
Take time to check gauge.

NOTES
1) When changing colors, pick up new color from under dropped color to prevent holes.
2) Carry color not in use, loosely across WS of work.

STITCH GLOSSARY
inc Knit into front and back of stitch.

HAT
Crown
With dpn and A, cast on 12 sts, leaving a long tail for sewing. Divide sts over 3 needles. Join taking care not to twist sts on needles, pm for beg of rnds.
Next 3 rnds Knit.
Next (inc) rnd *K2, inc in next st; rep from * around—16 sts.

Next rnd Knit.
Beg chart I (see page 91)
Rnd 1 Work 4-st pat rep 4 times. Cont to foll chart in this manner through rnd 2. Cont with A as foll:
Next rnd Knit.
Next (inc) rnd *K1, inc in next st; rep from * around—24 sts.
Next rnd Knit.
Beg chart II
Rnd 1 Work 4-st pat rep 6 times. Cont to foll chart in this manner through rnd 3. Cont with A as foll:
Next rnd Knit.
Next (inc) rnd *K1, inc in next st; rep from * around—36 sts.
Next rnd Knit.
Beg chart III
Rnd 1 Work 4-st pat rep 9 times. Cont to foll chart in this manner through rnd 3. Cont with A as foll:
Next rnd Knit.
Next (inc) rnd *K2, inc in next st; rep from * around—48 sts.
Next rnd Knit.
Beg chart IV
Rnd 1 Work 8-st pat rep 6 times. Cont to foll chart in this manner through rnd 4. Cont with A as foll:
Next rnd Knit.
Next (inc) rnd *K3, inc in next st; rep from * around—60 sts.
Next rnd Knit.
Beg chart V
Rnd 1 Work 4-st pat rep 15 times. Cont to foll chart in this manner through rnd 4. Cont with A as foll:
Next rnd Knit.
Next (inc) rnd *K4, inc in next st; rep from * around—72 sts.
Next rnd Knit. (Continued on page 91.)

lively

MATERIALS

Yarn
Bulky **by Blue Sky Alpacas,**
3½oz/100g balls, each approx
45yd/41m (alpaca/wool)
• **3 balls in #1104 polar bear**

Needles
• **One pair size 15 (10mm)**
needles or size to
obtain gauge
• **Two size 15 (10mm)**
double-pointed needles
(dpns) for I-cord

TIED HOODIE HAT

This peaked hood is perfect for a snow
queen in Narnia, but who wouldn't want
to tie it on when the cold winds set in?
An I-cord tie threaded through yarn
overs makes this bonnet extra-snug.

SIZE
One size fits all.

FINISHED MEASUREMENTS
Approx 8½"/21.5cm deep x 11"/28cm high
(excluding tie)

GAUGE
8 sts and 12 rows to 4"/10cm over St st
using size 15 (10mm) circular needle.
Take time to check gauge.

NOTE
Hat is made from the front edge to the
back (seam) edge.

STITCH GLOSSARY
3-needle bind-off
1) With WS tog, hold piece on two
parallel needles. Insert 3rd needle
knitwise into first st of each needle and
wrap yarn around needle as if to knit.
2) Knit these 2 sts tog and sl them off
the needles. *K the next 2 sts tog in the
same manner.
3) Sl first st on 3rd needle over the 2nd
st and off the needle. Rep from * in step
2 across row until all sts are bound off.

HAT
Beg at front edge, cast on 40 sts.
Row 1 (RS) Knit.
Row 2 Purl.
Row 3 Knit.

Row 4 Purl across, casting on 4 sts at
end of row—44 sts.
Row 5 Knit across, casting on 4 sts at
end of row—48 sts.
Row 6 Purl.
Row 7 (eyelets) K2, yo, k2tog, [k3, p3]
6 times, k3, p1, ssk, yo, k2.
Row 8 Knit the k sts and purl the p sts.
Row 9 K4, p1, [k3, p3] 6 times, k7.
Row 10 Rep row 8.
Row 11 K4, p2, [k3, p3] 6 times, k6.
Row 12 Rep row 8.
Row 13 (eyelets) K2, yo, k2tog, [p3, k3]
6 times, p3, k1, ssk, yo, k2.
Row 14 Rep row 8.
Row 15 K5, [p3, k3] 6 times, p3, k4.
Row 16 Rep row 8.
Row 17 K6, [p3, k3] 6 times, p2, k4.
Row 18 Rep row 8. Rep rows 7–18 once
more. Place first 24 sts on first needle;
leave rem 24 sts on 2nd needle. Using a
dpn for 3rd needle, cont to work 3-needle
bind-off.

I-CORD TIE
With dpn, cast on 3 sts, leaving a long
tail for sewing. Work in I-cord as foll:
Next row (RS) With 2nd dpn, k3, do
not turn. Slide sts back to beg of needle
to work next row from RS; rep from *
until I-cord measures 36"/91.5cm from
beg. Cut yarn, leaving a 6"/15.5cm tail.
Thread tail into tapestry needle, then
thread through rem sts. Pull tog tightly
and secure end. Thread beg tail in
tapestry needle. Weave tail around
opening at beg of I-cord. Pull tog tightly
and secure end. Weave I-cord through
eyelets. ❖

austere

MATERIALS

Yarn

Creative Focus Chunky by Nashua Handknits/Westminster Fibers, Inc, 3½oz/100g balls, each approx 110yd/100m (wool/alpaca)
• 2 balls in #410 nickel (A)

La Gran by Classic Elite Yarns, 1½oz/42g balls, each approx 90yd/82m (mohair/wool/nylon)
• 2 balls in #6539 eucalyptus green (B)

Kidsilk Haze by Rowan/Westminster Fibers, Inc., .88oz/25g balls, each approx 229yd/210m (super kid mohair/silk)
• 1 ball each in #588 drab (C) and #592 heavenly (D)

Needles

• Size 10½ (6.5mm) circular needles, 16"/40cm and 24"/61cm long or size to obtain gauge
• One set (4) size 10½ (6.5mm) double-pointed needles (dpns)
• Size 6 (4mm) circular needle, 24"/61cm long or size to obtain gauge

Notions

• Stitch marker

SCARF HAT

Although this hat would have made Heathcliff swoon even more if he saw Catherine wearing it, it's just as stylish on the streets of New York with the right coat or cape.

SIZES

Medium (Large)

FINISHED MEASUREMENTS

Hat
Circumference 22 (24)"/56 (61)cm
Scarf
Approx 52"/132cm long x 6½"/16.5cm wide

GAUGES

10 sts and 22 rnds to 4"/10cm over St st using larger circular needle and A and B yarns held tog (before felting).
14 sts and 34 rows to 4"/10cm over garter st using smaller circular needle and C (or D). **Take time to check gauges.**

NOTE

Use A and B held tog throughout.

STITCH GLOSSARY

inc Knit into front and back of stitch.

HAT

Crown

With dpn and A and B held tog, cast on 12 sts, leaving long tails for sewing. Divide sts over 3 needles. Join, taking care not to twist sts on needles, pm for beg of rnds.
Rnd 1 and all odd rnds Knit.
Rnd 2 *K1, inc in next st; rep from * around—18 sts.
Rnd 4 *K2, inc in next st; rep from * around—24 sts.

Rnd 6 *K3, inc in next st; rep from * around—30 sts.
Rnd 8 *K4, inc in next st; rep from * around—36 sts. Cont to work one more k st before inc every other rnd 4 (5) times more—60 (66) sts. Knit next rnd. Change to shorter circular needle.
Rise
Cont in St st until piece measures 9 (10)"/23 (25.5)cm from top of crown.
Brim
Change to longer circular needle. Drop B and cont with A only as foll:
Next (inc) rnd *K1, inc in next st; rep from * around—90 (99) sts. Knit next 6 rnds. Bind off all sts loosely.

SCARF

With smaller circular needle and C, cast on 190 sts loosely. Work back and forth in garter st for 3¼"/8cm from beg. Change to D. Cont in garter st for 3¼"/8cm. Bind off loosely knitwise.

FINISHING

Thread beg tails into tapestry needle. Weave tails around opening at top of crown. Pull tog tightly and secure ends.
Felting
Place hat in washing machine set to hot wash/cold rinse with low water level. Also add a pair of jeans for abrasion and balanced agitation. Add 1 tablespoon dishwashing detergent and ¼ cup baking soda at beginning of wash cycle. Repeat the cycle, if necessary, until hat is felted to finished measurement. Hand-block to shape, rolling up brim. Let air-dry. Using very sharp scissors, make a 1"/2.5cm horizontal slit on each side of hat (over each ear) just above beg of brim. Insert ends of scarf into slits. ❧

poetic

MATERIALS

Yarn
Bulky **by Blue Sky Alpacas,**
3½oz/100g hanks, each approx
45yd/41m (alpaca/wool)
- 1 hank in #1009 bobcat (A)
- 2 hanks in #1006 brown bear (B)

Needles
- **Two size 11 (8mm) circular needles, 16"/40cm long**
or size to obtain gauge
- **One set (4) size 11 (8mm) double-pointed needles (dpns)**

Notions
- **Stitch marker**

LUMBERJACK HAT

Not your brother's hat—but it could be. For the tomboy in you, what could be more practical to make or wear than this rugged flapped cap?

SIZES

One size fits all.

FINISHED MEASUREMENTS

Circumference 21½"/54.5cm

GAUGE

10 sts and 14 rnds to 4"/10cm over St st using size 11 (8mm) circular needle.
Take time to check gauge.

STITCH GLOSSARY

inc Knit into front and back of stitch.

GARTER STITCH

Rnd 1 Knit.
Rnd 2 Purl.
Rep rnds 1 and 2 for garter st ITR.

HAT

Crown
With dpn and A, cast on 12 sts, leaving a long tail for sewing. Divide sts over 3 needles. Join, taking care not to twist sts on needles, pm for beg of rnds.
Rnd 1 and all odd rnds Knit.
Rnd 2 *K1, inc in next st; rep from * around—18 sts.
Rnd 4 *K2, inc in next st; rep from * around—24 sts.
Rnd 6 *K3, inc in next st; rep from * around—30 sts.
Rnd 8 *K4, inc in next st; rep from * around—36 sts.
Rnd 10 *K5, inc in next st; rep from * around—42 sts.
Rnd 12 *K6, inc in next st; rep from * around—48 sts.
Rnd 14 *K7, inc in next st; rep from * around—54 sts.
Change to circular needle.
Rise
Cont in St st until piece measures 7"/17.5cm from top of crown.
Brim
Change to B. Cont in garter st for 12 rnds.
Front flap
Next row With dpn, k first 16 sts, leave rem 38 sts on circular needle. Using 2 dpns, work back and forth in garter st for 18 rows. Bind off loosely knitwise.
Back flap
Next row With RS facing, join B. Using 2 circular needles, work back and forth in garter st for 14 rows. Bind off loosely knitwise.

FINISHING

Thread beg tail into tapestry needle. Weave tail around opening at top of crown. Pull tog tightly and secure end. Fold front and back brims over to RS along the 6th garter st ridge. Tack corners of front flap to hat.❖

down-to-earth

MATERIALS

Yarn
Zara Plus **by Filatura Di Crosa/Tahki•Stacy Charles, Inc.**, 1¾oz/50g balls, each approx 77yd/70m (extrafine merino wool)
- 2 (3) balls in #26 red (MC)
- 1 (2) balls in #418 purple (CC)

Needles
- **Two size 7 (4.5mm) circular needles, 16"/40cm long** or size to obtain gauge
- **Size 7 (4.5mm) circular needle, 24"/61cm long**
- **One set (4) size 7 (4.5mm) double-pointed needles (dpns)**

Notions
- **Stitch marker**

RIPPLED CAP

A bold color combination for a strong personality. Traditional ruffles would have been too girly-girl, so a similar, but less fussy embellishment was used—think "waves." Each "wave" is knit separately and outlined with a contrasting color, then knit onto the main hat form.

SIZES

Medium (Large)

FINISHED MEASUREMENTS

Circumference 19⅝ (22)"/49.5 (56)cm

GAUGE

17 sts and 20 rnds to 4"/10cm over St st using size 7 (4.5mm) circular needle.
Take time to check gauge.

HAT

With longer circular needle and CC, cast on 168 (188) sts, leaving a long tail for sewing. Change to shorter circular needle and MC.
Next rnd *K2tog tbl; rep from * around—84 (94) sts. Join, taking care not to twist sts on needle, pm for beg of rnds. Knit next 6 rnds. Do not cut MC. Set aside.
**Make ruffle
With longer circular needle and CC, cast on 168 (188) sts, leaving a long tail for sewing. Change to shorter circular needle and MC.
Next rnd *K2tog tbl; rep from * around—84 (94) sts. Join, taking care not to twist sts on needle, pm for beg of rnds. Knit next 2 rnds. Cut MC.
Join ruffle to hat
Place ruffle over hat, so needles are parallel.
Next (joining) rnd K first st on each needle tog, cont to k2tog to end—84 (94) sts. With MC, knit next 4 rnds. Rep from ** (make ruffle) 5 times more, knitting only 2 rnds after last ruffle is joined.
Crown
Work in k1, p1 rib for 10 (14) rnds. Change to dpns.
Next (dec) rnd *K2tog tbl; rep from * around—42 (48) sts. Knit next 3 (4) rnds. Rep last 4 (5) rnds once more—21 (24) sts. Knit next 3 (4) rnds.
Next (dec) rnd *K2tog tbl; rep from * around, end k 1 (0)—11 (12) sts. Cut yarn, leaving a 6"/15.5cm tail. Thread tail into tapestry needle, then thread through rem sts. Pull tog tightly and secure end.

FINISHING

Sew side edges of CC cast-ons together.♣

confident

MATERIALS

Yarn
Swirl Chunky **by Lorna's Laces,
4oz/113g hanks, each approx
120yd/110m** (merino/silk)
- **3 hanks in #308 huron**

Needles
- **Size 10½ (6.5mm) circular
needles, 16"/40cm, 24"/60cm and
29"/75cm long** or size to obtain
gauge
- **One set (4) size 10½ (6.5mm)
double-pointed needles (dpns)**

Notions
- **Stitch marker**
- **One 2"/50mm button**

LOOP STITCH HELMET

This design may have been inspired by
1960s bathing caps with their loops,
leaves, flowers and appliqués, but this
bold, modern knit is better fit for an
urban warrior than a bathing beauty.
The "loop stitch" texture softens the
effect and adds a touch of humor.

SIZES
Medium (Large)

FINISHED MEASUREMENTS
Circumference 19½ (22)"/49.5 (56)cm

GAUGE
11 sts and 16 rnds to 4"/10cm over loop
st using size 10½(6.5mm) circular needle
and yarn held doubled.
Take time to check gauge.

NOTE
1) Yarn is held double throughout.
2) Brim and rise of hat are worked from
the WS. Crown is worked from the RS.

STITCH GLOSSARY
Make Loop (ML) Knit next st but do not
drop it from LH needle, bring yarn to
front between needles and wind it
around thumb. Take yarn to back
between needles and k the same st once
more tbl, slipping st off LH needle. Pass
the 2nd st on RH needle over the first st.

LOOP STITCH
Rnd 1 (RS) *ML in next st; rep from *
around.
Rnd 2 (RS) Knit.
Rep rnds 1 and 2 for loop st.

HAT

Brim and chin strap
With longest circular needle and 2
strands held tog, cast on 132 (138) sts.
Do not join.

Rnd 1 Bind off 78 sts (for chin strap),
change to 24"/60cm circular needle and k
to end—54 (60) sts on needle. Join,
taking care not to twist sts on needle, pm
for beg of rnds. Working with WS
facing, cont as foll:
Rnd 2 Purl.
Rnd 3 Knit.
Rnd 4 Purl.
Rise
Rep rnds 1 and 2 of loop st 6 times.
Crown
Rnd 1 Purl.
Rnd 2 Knit.
Rnd 3 Purl.
Rnd (dec) 4 *K4, k2tog tbl; rep from *
around—45 (50) sts.
Rnds 5–7 Rep rnds 1–3. Change to dpns.
Dec rnd 8 *K3, k2tog tbl; rep from *
around—36 (40) sts.
Rnds 9–11 Rep rnds 1–3.
Dec rnd 12 *K2, k2tog tbl; rep from *
around—27 (30) sts.
Rnds 13–15 Rep rnds 1–3.
Change to dpn.
Dec rnd 16 *K1, k2tog tbl; rep from *
around—18 (20) sts.
Rnd 17 Purl.
Dec rnd 18 [K2tog tbl] 9 (10) times—9
(10) sts. Cut yarn leaving 6"/15.5cm tails.
Thread tails into tapestry needle, then
thread through rem sts. Pull tog tightly
and secure ends.

FINISHING
Fold chin strap in half and align cast-on
edge together. Beg 1"/2.5cm from folded
end (button loop), whipstitch cast-on
edges together. Sew end of strap to
bottom edge of brim. On opposite side
of brim, sew on button, positioning it so
bottom edge of button extends ¼"/.5cm
below bottom edge of brim. ❖

MATERIALS

Yarn
Cashmerino **by Debbie Bliss/KFI,**
1¾oz/50g balls, each approx
125yd/114m(merino/microfiber/
cashmere)
- **2 balls in #4 red**

Needles
- **One pair size 8 (5mm)**
needles or size to obtain gauge
- **Size 8 (5mm) circular needles,**
16"/40cm and 24"/61cm long

Notions
- **Stitch marker**

LACY BALACLAVA

You're not taking any chances with the weather when you batten down the hatches in this cozy number. Knit in stop-sign red, it puts an end to the cold. Starting at the tippy-top, the hat is worked back and forth down the lacy part and is then joined to finish the neck in the round. Finally, stitches are picked up to make a ribbed facial "brim," which is folded over but can also be worn outward in inclement weather.

SIZE

One size fits all.

FINISHED MEASUREMENTS

Approx 9½"/24cm deep x 10½"/26.5cm high (excluding collar)

GAUGE

14 sts and 20 rows to 4"/10cm over St st using size 8 (5mm) circular needle.
Take time to check gauge.

VINE STITCH

(worked back and forth; multiple of 9 sts plus 2)
Row 1 (RS) K1, *k1, yo, k2, SKP, k2tog, k2, yo; rep from *, end k1.
Row 2 Purl.
Row 3 K1, *yo, k2, SKP, k2tog, k2, yo, k1; rep from *, end k2 instead of k1.
Row 4 Purl.
Rep rows 1–4 for vine st.

VINE STITCH

(worked ITR; multiple of 9 sts)
Rnd 1 *K1, yo, k2, SKP, k2tog, k2, yo; rep from * around.
Rnd 2 Knit.

Rnd 3 *Yo, k2, SKP, k2tog, k2, yo, k1; rep from * around.
Rnd 4 Knit.
Rep rnds 1–4 for vine st.

HAT

With straight needles, cast on 65 sts. Work back and forth in vine st for 9"/23cm, end on row 3.
Next (dec) row (WS) P2tog, p to last 2 sts, p2tog—63 sts.
Neck (worked ITR)
Change to shorter circular needle. With RS of vine st facing, join to work ITR as foll:
Next rnd Work rnd 1 of vine st (ITR), casting on 9 sts at end of rnd—72 sts. Cont in vine st for 11 rnds more.
Collar
Rnds 1–6 *K2, p2; rep from * around.
Rnd 7 *K1, m1, k1, p2; rep from * around—90 sts.
Rnd 8 *K3, p2; rep from * around.
Rnd 9 *[K1, m1] twice, k1, p2; rep from * around—126 sts.
Rnds 10–16 *K5, p2; rep from * around.
Bind off loosely in rib pat.

FINISHING

Sew top seam.
Front band
With RS facing, longer circular needle, beg at center st of 9 sts cast-on, pick up and k 40 sts evenly spaced along front edge to top seam, pick up and k 40 sts to the end—80 sts. Join and pm for beg of rnds.
Rnds 1–3 *K2, p2; rep from * around.
Rnd 4 *K1, m1, k1, p2; rep from * around—100 sts.
Rnds 5–14 *K3, p2; rep from * around.
Bind off loosely in rib pat. ♣

cautious

MATERIALS

Yarn
Cashsoft Aran **by Rowan/
Westminster Fibers, Inc.,**
1¾oz/50g balls, each approx
95yd/87m (extrafine merino/
acrylic microfiber/cashmere)
• **4 balls in #1 oat**

Needles
• **One set (4) size 6 (4mm)
double-pointed needles (dpns)**
or size to obtain gauge

Notions
• **Stitch marker**
• **Eleven 12mm pearls**
• **Sewing needle**
• **Matching sewing thread**

LEAF MOTIF HEADBAND

Although the Romans hardly had need of
winter wear—they left for the resort of
Pompeii when temperatures dipped—a
crown of laurel leaves was considered *de
rigueur* for the highest in the land. This
one's fit for today's noblewoman. The head-
band is worked in the round, and while the
texture of the leaves require a bit of focus,
it's well worth the effort.

SIZE
One size fits all.

FINISHED MEASUREMENTS
Approx 5"/12.5cm wide x 19½"/49.5cm
long (excluding ties)

GAUGE
24 sts and 32 rnds to 4"/10cm over St st
using size 6 (4mm) dpns.
Take time to check gauge.

STITCH GLOSSARY
inc Knit into front and back of stitch.

HEADBAND
First tie
With dpn, cast on 12 sts, leaving a long
tail for sewing. Divide sts over 3 needles.
Join, taking care not to twist sts on
needles, pm for beg of rnds. Work around
in St st for 15"/38cm.
Next rnd K6, pm, k to end.
Side shaping
Rnd 1 For front, k1, m1, p to 1 st before
next marker (front sts), m1, k1, sl
marker, for back, k1, m1, p to 1 st before
next marker (back sts), m1, k1—16 sts.
Rnd 2 K2, p to 2 sts before next marker,
k2, sl marker, k2, p to 2 sts before next
marker, k2.
Rnd 3 Rep rnd 1—20 sts.

Rnd 4 Rep rnd 2.
Rnd 5 Rep rnd 1—24 sts.
Rnd 6 Rep rnd 2.
Rnd 7 K1, m1, p3, k4, p3, m1, k1, sl
marker, k1, m1, p to 1 st before marker,
m1, k1—28 sts.
Rnd 8 K2, p3, k4, p3, k2, sl marker, k2, p
to 2 sts before next marker, k2.
Rnd 9 K1, m1, p4, k4, p4, m1, k1, sl
marker, k1, m1, p to 1 st before marker,
m1, k1—32 sts.
Rnd 10 K2, p4, k4, p4, k2, sl marker, k2, p
to 2 sts before next marker, k2.
Rnd 11 K1, m1, p5, k1, k2tog, k1, p5,
m1, k1, sl marker, k1, m1, p to 1 st
before marker, m1, k1—35 sts.
Rnd 12 K2, p5, k3, p5, k2, sl marker, k2, p
to 2 sts before next marker, k2.
Rnd 13 K1, m1, p6, k3, p6, m1, k1, sl
marker, k1, m1, p to 1 st before marker,
m1, k1—39 sts.
Rnd 14 K2, p5, [k1, p1] twice, k1, p5, k2,
sl marker, k2, p to 2 sts before next
marker, k2.
Rnd 15 K1, m1, p4, p2tog, [yo, p1] twice,
k1, [p1, yo] twice, p2tog, p4, m1, k1, sl
marker, k1, m1, p to 1 st before marker,
m1, k1—45 sts.
Rnd 16 K2, p5, k3, inc in next st, k1, inc in
next st, k3, p5, k2, sl marker, k2, p to 2 sts
before next marker, k2—47 sts.
Rnd 17 K1, m1, p4, p2tog, [k1, yo] twice,
k1, p2, k1, p2, [k1, yo] twice, k1, p2tog,
p4, M1, k1, sl marker, k1, m1, p to 1 st
before marker, m1, k1—53 sts.
Rnd 18 K2, p5, k5, p1, inc in next st, k1,
inc in next st, p1, k5, p5, k2, sl marker, k2,
p to 2 sts before next marker, k2—55 sts.
Rnd 19 K1, m1, p4, p2tog, k2, yo, k1, yo,
k2, p3, k1, p3, k2, yo, k1, yo, k2, p2tog,
(Continued on page 92.)

MATERIALS

Yarn
Baby Alpaca Grande Tweed **by Plymouth Yarn Company**, 3½oz/100g hanks, each approx 110yd/100m (baby alpaca & acrylic/polyester)
• 1 hank in #5298 mint (MC)
Baby Alpaca Grande **by Plymouth Yarn Company**, 3½oz/100g hanks, each approx 110yd/100m (baby alpaca)
• 1 hank in #302 chocolate (CC)

Needles
• **One size 10 (6mm) circular needle, 16"/40cm long** or size to obtain gauge
• **One set (4) size 10 (6mm) double-pointed needles (dpns)**

Notions
• **Stitch marker**

PONYTAIL HAT

Not exactly a bad-hair-day hat, but it's just the solution for those with long tresses looking for a way to have a ponytail but wear a hat too. The crown is worked in-the-round from the top down, but once the rise begins it's worked back and forth to allow for the back opening.

SIZES
Medium (Large)

FINISHED MEASUREMENTS
Circumference 18½ (20½)"/47 (52)cm

GAUGES
14 sts and 20 rnds to 4"/10cm over St st using size 10 (6mm) circular needle and MC.
13 sts and 24 rows to 4"/10cm over seed st using size 10 (6mm) circular needle and MC.
Take time to check gauges.

STITCH GLOSSARY
inc Knit into front and back of stitch.

SEED STITCH
(multiple of 2 sts)
Row 1 *K1, p1; rep from * around.
Row 2 Knit the p sts and purl the k sts.
Rep row 2 for seed st.

HAT
Crown
With dpns and MC, cast on 12 sts, leaving a long tail for sewing. Divide sts over 3 needles. Join, taking care not to twist sts on needles, pm for beg of rnds.
Rnd 1 and all odd rnds Knit.
Rnd 2 *K1, inc in next st; rep from * around—18 sts.
Rnd 4 *K2, inc in next st; rep from * around—24 sts.
Rnd 6 *K3, inc in next st; rep from * around—30 sts.
Rnd 8 *K4, inc in next st; rep from * around—36 sts. Cont to work one more k st before inc every other rnd 4 (5) times more—60 (66) sts. Change to circular needle. Knit next rnd. Turn work.

Rise
Working back and forth on circular needle, work even in seed st for 4½(5)"/11.5 (12.5)cm. Cut MC, leaving a long tail. Set aside.

I-cord edging and tie
For first tie, with dpn and CC, cast on 3 sts leaving a long tail. Work in I-cord as foll: ***Next row (RS)** With 2nd dpn, k3, do not turn. Slide sts back to beg of needle to work next row from RS; rep from * until I-cord measures 4"/10cm from beg. Do not slide sts back to beg of needle. With RS of hat facing and working from right to left, apply I-cord to hat edge as foll: With RS facing, slip the 3 sts from dpn to beg of circular needle. ***Next row** With dpn and CC, k2, k2tog tbl (this includes MC st). Return the 3 sts to circular needle as before; rep from * until all sts from circular needle have been worked. For 2nd tie, cont in I-cord for 4"/10cm. Cut yarn, leaving a long tail. Thread tail into tapestry needle, then weave needle through sts. Pull tail to gather; fasten off securely. Rep for first tie.

FINISHING
Thread beg tail in tapestry needle. Weave tail around opening at top of crown. Pull tog tightly and secure end. Knot each end of I-cord in an overhand knot, then tie in a square knot to fasten edging together. ❧

MATERIALS

Yarn
Supercotton **by Schulana/Skacel Collection, Inc., 1¾oz/50g balls, each approx 98yd/90m (cotton/polyester)**
• **3 balls in #20 off-white**

Needles
• **Size 10½ (6.5mm) circular needle, 16"/40cm long** or size to obtain gauge
• **One set (4) size 10½ (6.5mm) double-pointed needles (dpns)**

Notions
• **Stitch marker**
• **300 (330) ¾"/20mm gold paillettes with large holes**

SPANGLED HAT

Some might think sequins and spangles are just for galas, but not you. What better way to boost the spirits and match your sparkling personality? The large sequins (paillettes) have to be pre-strung before you begin work. After the crown is formed the spangles are taken up one by one, a stitch at a time. It might just be time to party when you're through.

SIZES
Medium (Large)

FINISHED MEASUREMENTS
Circumference 20 (22)"/51 (56)cm

GAUGE
12 sts and 20 rnds to 4"/10cm over St st using size 10½ (6.5mm) circular needle and yarn held doubled.
Take time to check gauge.

PAILLETTE PATTERN
Rnd 1 *K1, slide paillette up, hold in front and place next to st on RH needle; rep from * around.
Rnds 2–4 Knit.
Rep rnds 1–4 for paillette pat.

NOTES
Yarn is held double throughout.

STITCH GLOSSARY
inc Knit into front and back of stitch.

HAT
Thread 2 strands of yarn in tapestry needle. Thread all paillettes onto double strand of yarn.
Crown
With dpn and 2 strands held tog, cast on 12 sts, leaving long tails for sewing.

Divide sts over 3 needles. Join and pm, taking care not to twist sts on needles.
Rnd 1 and all odd rnds Knit.
Rnd 2 *K1, inc 1 in next st; rep from * around—18 sts.
Rnd 4 *K2, inc 1 in next st; rep from * around—24 sts.
Rnd 6 *K3, inc 1 in next st; rep from * around—30 sts.
Rnd 8 *K4, inc 1 in next st; rep from * around—36 sts.
Rnd 10 *K5, inc 1 in next st; rep from * around—42 sts.
Rnd 12 *K6, inc 1 in next st; rep from * around—48 sts.
Rnd 14 *K7, inc 1 in next st; rep from * around—54 sts.
Rnd 16 *K8, inc 1 in next st; rep from * around—60 sts.
For Large size only
Rnd 17 Knit.
Rnd 18 *K9, inc 1 in next st; rep from * around—66 sts.
For both sizes
Change to circular needle. Form turning ridge as foll:
Rnd 1 Knit.
Rnds 2 and 3 Purl.
Rnd 4 Knit.
Rise
Rep rnds 1–4 of paillette pat 4 times, then rep rnd 1 once.
Brim
Rnds 1 and 2 Knit.
Rnds 3–7 Purl. Bind off all sts loosely knitwise.

FINISHING
Thread beg tails in tapestry needle. Weave tails around opening at top of crown. Pull tog tightly and secure ends. ❖

flirtatious

MATERIALS

Yarn
Zara Chiné **by Filatura Di Crosa/
Tahki•Stacy Charles, Inc.,
1¾oz/50g balls, each approx
137yd/125m (merino wool)**
• **3 balls in #1709 light denim
chiné (A)**
New Smoking **by Filatura Di
Crosa/Tahki•Stacy Charles,
Inc., .88oz/25g balls, each
approx 132yd/120m
(viscose/polyester)**
• **2 balls in #2 silver (B)**

Needles
• **Size 10 (6mm) circular needle,
16"/40cm long** or size to obtain
gauge
• **One set (4) size 10 (6mm)
double-pointed needles (dpns)**

Notions
• **Stitch marker**

CHECKERBOARD HAT
A cool-as-ice blue and silver hat for those
days when you just want to be left alone. Be
careful, though—the fun pattern, mood-
lifting extended rise and glints of metallic
yarn might raise your spirits!

SIZES
Medium (Large)

FINISHED MEASUREMENTS
Circumference 19 (20½)"/48 (52)cm

GAUGE
14 sts and 20 rnds to 4"/10cm over
checkerboard pat using size 10 (6mm)
circular needle and A and B held tog.
Take time to check gauge.

NOTE
Use A and B held tog throughout.

STITCH GLOSSARY
inc Knit into front and back of stitch.

CHECKERBOARD PATTERN
(multiple of 6 sts)
Rnds 1–4 *K3, p3; rep from * around.
Rnds 5–8 *P3, k3; rep from * around.
Rep rnds 1–8 for checkerboard pat.

HAT
Crown
With dpn and A and B held tog, cast on
12 sts, leaving long tails for sewing.
Divide sts over 3 needles. Join, taking
care not to twist sts on needles, pm for
beg of rnds.
Rnd 1 and all odd rnds Knit.
Rnd 2 *K1, inc in next st; rep from *
around—18 sts.
Rnd 4 *K2, inc in next st; rep from *
around—24 sts.
Rnd 6 *K3, inc in next st; rep from *
around—30 sts.
Rnd 8 *K4, inc in next st; rep from *
around—36 sts.
Rnd 10 *K5, inc in next st; rep from *
around—42 sts.
Rnd 12 *K6, inc in next st; rep from *
around—48 sts.
Rnd 14 *K7, inc in next st; rep from *
around—54 sts.
Rnd 16 *K8, inc in next st; rep from *
around—60 sts.
Rnd 18 *K9, inc in next st; rep from *
around—66 sts.
For Large size only
Rnd 19 Knit.
Rnd 20 *K10, inc in next st; rep from *
around—72 sts.
For both sizes
Change to circular needle. Purl next 3
rnds for turning ridge.
Rise
Rep rnds 1–8 of checkerboard pat 4
times, then rnds 1–4 once.
Brim
Rnds 1–10 Knit.
Rnd 11 Purl.
Rnd 12 Knit. Bind off loosely knitwise.

FINISHING
Thread beg tails into tapestry needle.
Weave tails around opening at top of
crown. Pull tog tightly and secure ends.
Fold brim 1¾"/4.5cm over to RS. Using A
in tapestry needle, sew a running stitch
(see page 96) between rnds 10 and 11 of
brim, to secure brim in place. ✤

brooding

MATERIALS

Yarn
Bulky **by Blue Sky Alpacas,
3½oz/100g hanks, each
approx 45yd/41m (alpaca/
wool)**
• **1 hank in #1009 bobcat (A)**
Opulent **by Ozark Handspun,
3½oz/100g hanks, each
approx 50yd/46m (wool/
mohair)**
• **1 hank in #346 indian (B)**

Needles
• **One set (4) size 10½
(6.5mm) double-pointed
needles (dpns)** or size
to obtain gauge
• **Size 15 (10mm) circular
needle, 16"/40cm long**
or size to obtain gauge

Notions
• **Stitch marker**

TEXTURED PILLBOX

This hat is made for serious yarn lovers
intent on great color and texture. A
gorgeous hand-spun and dyed wool-
mohair blend is alternated with a soft,
nubby alpaca and wool yarn to create
just the right amount of texture. You
won't be able to hide your enthusiasm
for this luscious chapeau.

SIZES

Medium (Large)

FINISHED MEASUREMENTS

Circumference 21½ (22½)"/54.5 (57)cm

GAUGES

10 sts and 14 rnds to 4"/10cm over St st
using size 10½ (6.5mm) dpns and A.
7 sts and 12 rnds to 4"/10cm over St st
using size 15 (10mm) circular needle and
B. **Take time to check gauges.**

STITCH GLOSSARY

inc Knit into front and back of stitch.

HAT
Crown

With dpn and A, cast on 12 sts, leaving a
long tail for sewing. Divide sts over 3
needles. Join, taking care not to twist sts
on needles, pm for beg of rnds.

Rnd 1 *K1, inc in next st; rep from *
around—18 sts.
Rnd 2 and all even rnds Knit.
Rnd 3 *K2, inc in next st; rep from *
around—24 sts.
Rnd 5 *K3, inc in next st; rep from *
around—30 sts.
Rnd 7 *K4, inc in next st; rep from *
around—36 sts.
Rnd 9 *K17, inc in next st; rep from *
around—38 sts.
For Large size only
Rnd 9 *K8, inc in next st; rep from *
around—40 sts.
For both sizes
Knit next rnd. Turn crown WS (purl side)
out. Change to circular needle and B.
Rise
Rnds 1–5 With B, knit.
Rnd 6 With A, knit.
Rep rnds 1–6 twice more.
Brim
Rnds 1–3 With A, knit. Bind off loosely
knitwise. Turn hat inside out, so purl
side of sides and knit side of crown are
on RS.

FINISHING

Thread beg tail into tapestry needle.
Weave tail around opening at top of crown.
Pull tog tightly and secure end. ✤

earnest

MATERIALS

Yarn
Opulent **by Ozark Handspun,
3½oz/100g hanks, each
approx 50yd/46m (wool/mohair)**
• **1 hank in #143 sima (MC)**
Burley Spun **by Brown Sheep
Company, 8oz/226g hanks, each
approx 130yd/119m (wool)**
• **1 ball in #BS07 sable (CC)**

Needles
• **Size 13 (9mm) circular
needle, 16"/40cm long**
or size to obtain gauge
• **One set (4) size 13 (9mm)
double-pointed needles (dpns)**

Notions
• **Stitch marker**

FLOWERED CAP

With flecks of pinks and reds, this very
feminine hat evokes a field of flowers.
The crown is worked from the top down
and anchored with a chocolate brown
(and itch-free) brim band.

SIZES
Medium (Large)

FINISHED MEASUREMENTS
Circumference 19½ (21½)"/49.5 (54.5)cm

GAUGE
10 sts and 14 rnds to 4"/10cm over St
st using size 13 (9mm) circular needle
and MC.
Take time to check gauge.

STITCH GLOSSARY
inc Knit into front and back of stitch.

HAT
Crown
With dpn and MC, cast on 12 sts,
leaving a long tail for sewing. Divide sts
over 3 needles. Join, taking care not to
twist sts on needles, pm for beg of rnds.
Rnd 1 and all odd rnds Knit.
Rnd 2 *K1, inc in next st; rep from *
around—18 sts.

Rnd 4 *K2, inc in next st; rep from *
around—24 sts.
Rnd 6 *K3, inc in next st; rep from *
around—30 sts.
Rnd 8 *K4, inc in next st; rep from *
around—36 sts.
Rnd 10 *K5, inc in next st; rep from *
around—42 sts.
Rnd 12 *K6, inc in next st; rep from *
around—48 sts.
For Large size only
Rnd 13 Knit.
Rnd 14 *K7, inc in next st; rep from *
around—54 sts.
For both sizes
Change to circular needle.
Knit next rnd.
Brim
Turn crown WS (purl side) out.
This is now the RS. Change to CC.
Rnds 1 and 2 Knit.
Rnds 3 and 4 Purl. Rep rnds 1–4 once
more. Knit next rnd. Bind off loosely
knitwise.

FINISHING
Thread beg tail into tapestry needle.
Weave tail around opening
at top of crown. Pull tog tightly
and secure end. ❖

romantic

MATERIALS

Yarn
Classic Wool **by Paton Yarns**,
3½oz/100g balls, each approx
223yd/205m (wool)
- 1 ball in #208 jade heather (A)
- 1 ball in #240 leaf green (B)

Needles
- **Size 7 (4.5mm) circular needle, 16"/40cm long**
or size to obtain gauge
- **One set (4) size 7 (4.5mm) double-pointed needles (dpns)**

Notions
- **Stitch marker**

TWO-TONED TASSEL HAT

Vaguely reminiscent of a propeller hat, this flight of fancy is much more stylish and refined. After the basic hat is made—preferably in two colors to show off your I-cord work—segments of the ribbed brim are bound off, and the rest are continued with I-cord, which is gathered at the top. Instant fireworks!

SIZES
Medium (Large)

FINISHED MEASUREMENTS
Circumference 19½ (22)"/49.5 (56)cm

GAUGES
20 sts and 24 rnds to 4"/10cm over St st using size 7 (4.5mm) circular needle.
22 sts and 26 rnds to 4"/10cm over k3, p3 rib (slightly stretched) using size 7 (4.5mm) circular needle.
Take time to check gauges.

STITCH GLOSSARY
inc Knit into front and back of stitch.

HAT
Crown
With dpn and A, cast on 12 sts, leaving a long tail for sewing. Divide sts over 3 needles. Join, taking care not to twist sts on needles, pm for beg of rnds.
Rnd 1 and all odd rnds Knit.
Rnd 2 *K1, inc in next st; rep from * around—18 sts.
Rnd 4 *K2, inc in next st; rep from * around—24 sts.
Rnd 6 *K3, inc in next st; rep from * around—30 sts.
Rnd 8 *K4, inc in next st; rep from * around—36 sts.
Rnd 10 *K5, inc in next st; rep from * around—42 sts.

Rnd 12 *K6, inc in next st; rep from * around—46 sts.
Rnd 14 *K7, inc in next st; rep from * around—54 sts. Cont to work one more k st before inc every other rnd 9 (11) times more—108(120) sts. Change to circular needle. Work even for 3"/7.5cm. Change to B. Knit next rnd.
Brim
Cont in k3, p3 rib for 4 (4½)"/10 (11.5)cm. Turn piece WS out.
Next (bind off) rnd Sl 1, k2, *bind off next 3 p-sts, k2; rep from * around, using the first st of the next rnd to complete the last 3-st bind-off.
First I-cord
Place first 3 sts on circular needle on a dpn. Work in I-cord as foll:
*Next row (RS)** With 2nd dpn, k3, do not turn. Slide sts back to beg of needle to work next row from RS; rep from * until I-cord measures 11 (11½)"/28 (29)cm from beg. Cut yarn leaving a 6"/15.5cm tail. Thread tail in tapestry needle, then thread through rem sts. Pull tog tightly and secure end.
Second I-cord
Place next 3 sts on circular needle on a dpn. Join B and cont to work as for first I-cord. Cont in this manner until 16 (18) rem I-cords are completed.

FINISHING
Thread beg tail into tapestry needle. Weave tail around opening at top of crown. Pull tog tightly and secure end. Cut a 24"/61cm strand of B. Thread into tapestry needle and use doubled. Working 4½"/11.5cm from end of I-cords and from right to left, insert needle through each I-cord. Pull tog tightly, secure end but do not cut yarn. Wrap yarn twice around bundle and secure end.❖

whimsical

MATERIALS

Yarn
Montera **by Classic Elite Yarns,**
3½oz/100g hanks, each approx
127yd/116m (llama/wool)
• **1 hank in #3849 amethyst (A)**
La Gran **by Classic Elite Yarns,**
1½oz/42g balls, each approx
90yd/82m (mohair/wool/nylon)
• **2 balls in #61556 lovely lilac (B)**

Needles
• **Size 10½ (6.5mm) circular**
needle, 16"/40cm long
or size to obtain gauge
• **One set (4) size 10½ (6.5mm)**
double-pointed needles (dpns)

Notions
• **Stitch marker**
• **¾yd/.75m of ¾"/20mm-wide**
feather trim

FELTED FEDORA

This kicky high-top felted hat
complements a range of head sizes
and face shapes. You can personalize it
by changing the decoration on the
brim; try sequins, ribbons, a vintage
buckle, leather cord—you name it!

SIZES
Medium (Large)

FINISHED MEASUREMENTS
Circumference 22 (24)"/56 (61)cm

GAUGE
12 sts and 22 rnds to 4"/10cm over St st
using size 10½ (6.5mm) circular needle
and A and B held tog (before felting).
Take time to check gauge.

NOTE
Use A and B held tog throughout.

STITCH GLOSSARY
inc Knit into front and back of stitch.

HAT
Crown
With dpn and A and B held tog, cast on
12 sts, leaving long tails for sewing.
Divide sts over 3 needles. Join, taking
care not to twist sts on needles, pm for
beg of rnds.
Rnd 1 and all odd rnds Knit.
Rnd 2 *K1, inc in next st; rep from *
around—18 sts.
Rnd 4 *K2, inc in next st; rep from *
around—24 sts.
Rnd 6 *K3, inc in next st; rep from *
around—30 sts.
Rnd 8 *K4, inc in next st; rep from *
around—36 sts. Cont to work one more
k st before inc every other rnd 3 (4)
times more—54 (60) sts. Knit next rnd.
Change to circular needle.
Purl next 3 rnds for turning ridge.
Rise shaping
Rnds 1–4 Knit.
Rnd 5 *K 8 (9), inc in next st; rep from
* around—60 (66) sts.
Rnds 6–9 Knit.
Rnd 10 *K 9 (10), inc in next st; rep
from * around—66 (72) sts.
Rnds 11–14 Knit.
Rnd 15 *K 10 (11), inc in next st; rep
from * around—72 (78) sts.
Rnds 16–32 Knit.
Brim
Next (inc) rnd *K3, inc in next st; rep
from * around, end k 0 (2)—90 (97) sts.
Knit next 7 rnds. Bind off all sts
loosely.

FINISHING
Thread beg tails into tapestry needle.
Weave tails around opening at top
of crown. Pull tog tightly and secure
ends.
Felting
Place hat in washing machine set to
hot wash/cold rinse with low water
level. Also add a pair of jeans for
abrasion and balanced agitation. Add 1
tablespoon dishwashing detergent
and ¼ cup baking soda at beginning
of wash cycle. Repeat the cycle, if
necessary, until hat is felted to finished
measurement. Hand-block to shape,
rolling up brim. Let air-dry. Sew on
trim for hatband. ❧

Joyful

MATERIALS

Yarn

Glitterspun **by Lion Brand Yarn**, 1¾oz/50g skeins, each approx 115yd/105m (acrylic/cupro/polyester)
• 5 skeins in #170 gold

Needles
• Size 10 (6mm) circular needle, 16"/40cm long
or size to obtain gauge
• Cable needle (cn)

Notions
• Stitch marker

CABLED POMPOM HAT

For girls who just want to have fun, what's more cheeful than a hat knit with glittery gold yarn? Metallics are eternally in style. Start at the ribbed brim base and work upwards—then top it all off with a pompom for extra sparkle.

SIZES
Medium (Large)

FINISHED MEASUREMENTS
Circumference 18 (20)"/45.5 (50.5)cm

GAUGES
16 sts and 22 rnds to 4"/10cm over St st or k1, p1 rib (slightly stretched) using size 10 (6mm) circular needle and yarn held doubled.
26 sts to 5"/12.5cm over cable pat (stretched) using size 10 (6mm) circular needle and yarn held doubled.
Take time to check gauges.

NOTE
Yarn is held double throughout.

STITCH GLOSSARY
6-st LC Sl next 3 sts to cn and hold in *front*, k3, k3 from cn.

CABLE PATTERN
Rnds 1–3 K5 (7), [p2, k6] 3 times, p2, k10 (14), [p2, k6] 3 tmes, p2, k5 (7).
Rnd 4 K5 (7), p2, 6-st LC, p2, k6, p2, 6-st LC, p2, k10 (14), p2, 6-st LC, p2, k6, p2, 6-st LC, p2, k5 (7).
Rnds 5–7 Rep rnds 1–3.
Rnd 8 K5 (7), p2, k6, p2, 6-st LC, p2, k6, p2, k10 (14), p2, k6, p2, 6-st LC, p2, k6, p2, k5 (7).
Rep rnds 1–8 for cable pat.

HAT

Brim
With circular needle and 2 strands held tog, cast on 72 (80) sts. Join and pm, taking care not to twist sts on needle. Work around in k1, p1 rib for 4½"/11.5cm.

Rise
Rep rnds 1–8 of cable pat 6 times. Bind off in pat st.

FINISHING
Fold hat in half, matching cable sections, then sew top seam. Fold hat in half again, matching St st section, and forming two points. Sew tips of points together. Push fold up to joined points, then sew to underside of points.

Pompom
Make a 3½"/9cm-diameter pompom (See page 96). Sew to top of hat. Fold brim in half to RS. ✤

MATERIALS

Yarn
La Gran by Classic Elite Yarns, 1¼oz/42g balls, each approx 90yd/82m (mohair/wool/nylon)
• 1 ball in #6593 electric blue (A)
Lamb's Pride Bulky by Brown Sheep Company, 4oz/113g skeins, each approx 125yd/114m (wool/mohair)
• 1 skein each in #M05 onyx (B) and #M197 red hot passion (C)

Needles
• **Two size 10½ (6.5mm) circular needles, 16"/40cm long** or size to obtain gauge
• **One set (4) size 10½ (6.5mm) double-pointed needles (dpns)**

Notions
• **Stitch marker**
• **Tracing paper**

APPLIQUÉD PILLBOX

Idealism is never out of fashion. Make the star slightly imperfect to show it's a bit tongue-in-cheek.

SIZES
Medium (Large)

FINISHED MEASUREMENTS
Circumference 20 (22)"/51 (56)cm

GAUGE
10 sts and 20 rnds to 4"/10cm over St st using size 10½ (6.5mm) circular needle and A and B held tog (before felting).
Take time to check gauge.

NOTE
Use A and B held tog throughout.

STITCH GLOSSARY
inc Knit into front and back of stitch.

HAT
Crown
With dpns and A and B held tog, cast on 12 sts, leaving long tails for sewing. Divide sts over 3 needles. Join, taking care not to twist sts on needles, pm for beg of rnds.
Rnd 1 and all odd rnds Knit.
Rnd 2 *K1, inc in next st; rep from * around—18 sts.
Rnd 4 *K2, inc in next st; rep from * around—24 sts.
Rnd 6 *K3, inc in next st; rep from * around—30 sts.
Rnd 8 *K4, inc in next st; rep from * around—36 sts. Cont to work one more k st before inc every other rnd 5(6) times more—66 (72) sts. Knit next rnd. Change to circular needle. Purl next 3 rnds for turning ridge.
Rise
Cont to work even in St st for 5"/12.5cm.
Front flap
Next row With dpns, k first 18 sts, leave rem 48 (54) sts on circular needle. Using 2 dpns, work back and forth in St st for 5"/12.5cm. Bind off loosely knitwise.
Back flap
With RS facing, join A and B. Using 2 circular needles, work back and forth as foll:
Next (dec) row K2, k2tog, k to last 4 sts, k2tog, k2—46 (52) sts. Purl next row. Rep last 2 rows 3 times more—40 (46) sts. Bind off loosely knitwise as foll: [K2tog] twice, pass first st on RH needle over 2nd st, cont to bind off to last 4 sts, k2tog, bind off st, k2tog, bind off last st.

STAR APPLIQUÉ
With circular needle and C, cast on 24 sts. Work back and forth in St st for 6"/15cm. Bind off loosely knitwise.

FINISHING
Thread beg tails into tapestry needle. Weave tails around opening at top of crown. Pull tog tightly and secure ends.
Felting
Felt hat and star appliqué separately. Place hat in washing machine set to hot wash/cold rinse with low water level. Also add a pair of jeans for abrasion and balanced agitation. Add 1 tablespoon dishwashing detergent and ¼ cup baking soda at beginning of wash cycle. Repeat the cycle, if necessary, until hat is felted to finished measurement. Hand-block to pillbox shape, folding up front flap. Let air-dry. Repeat felting technique for star appliqué. Block piece flat. Tack front flap to hat at each top corner.
Star appliqué
Trace actual-size pattern for star (see page 93) on tracing paper. Cut out pattern. Pin pattern to felted piece. Cut out using sharp scissors. Referring to photo, position star so it overlaps right edge of front flap, and top and right points of star overlap top of hat. Using a single strand of C in tapestry needle, secure star point in place with a French knot. ✦

idealistic

MATERIALS

Yarn
Aspen **by Classic Elite Yarns, 3.5oz/100g hanks, each approx 51yd/47m** (alpaca/wool)
• **2 hanks in #1575 latte**

Needles
• **Size 11 (8mm) circular needle, 16"/40cm long**
or size to obtain gauge
• **One set (4) size 11 (8mm) double-pointed needles (dpns)**
• **Cable needle (cn)**

Notions
• **Stitch marker**

CABLED VISOR CAP

Always chic, visor caps are simpler to make than they might look. The hat is worked from the top down in the round in a richly textured pattern, then back and forth with decreases on either side to gradually form the visor. Try it and you'll be a believer.

SIZES
Medium (Large)

FINISHED MEASUREMENTS
Circumference 19 (22½)"/48 (57)cm

GAUGE
10 sts and 20 rnds to 4"/10cm over cable pat using size 11 (8mm) circular needle. Take time to check gauge.

STITCH GLOSSARY
inc Knit into front and back of stitch.
2-st LPC Sl 1 st to cn and hold in *front*, p1, k1 st from cn.
2-st RPC Sl 1 st to cn and hold in *back*, k1, p1 from cn.

CABLE PATTERN
(multiple of 4 sts)
Rnds 1 and 2 *K1, p2, k1; rep from * around.
Rnd 3 *2-st LPC, 2-st RPC; rep from * around.
Rnds 4–7 *P1, k2, p1; rep from * around.
Rnd 8 *2-st RPC, 2-st LPC; rep from * around.
Rnds 9 and 10 *K1, p2, k1; rep from * around.
Rep rnds 1–10 for cable pat.

HAT
Crown
With dpn and A, cast on 12 sts, leaving a long tail for sewing. Divide sts over 3 needles. Join, taking care not to twist sts on needles, pm for beg of rnds.
Rnd 1 Knit.
Rnd 2 [Inc in next st] 12 times—24 sts.
Rnd 3 Knit.
Rnd 4 [Inc in next st] 24 times—48 sts.
Rnd 5 Knit.
For Large size only
Rnd 6 *K5, inc in next st; rep from * around—56 sts.
Rnd 7 Knit.
For both sizes
Change to circular needle.
Rise
Rep rnds 1–10 of cable pat twice, then rnds 1–5 once. Purl next rnd, dropping marker.
Visor
You will be working back and forth using 2 dpns and 2 strands of yarn held tog as foll:
Row 1 (RS) K17 (19); turn.
Row 2 K16 (18); turn.
Row 3 K15 (17); turn.
Row 4 K14 (16); turn.
Row 5 K13 (15); turn.
Row 6 K12 (14); turn.
Row 7 K11 (13); turn.
Row 8 K10 (12); turn.
Row 9 K9 (11); turn.
Row 10 K8 (10); turn. Change to circular needle and one strand of yarn. Pm on RH needle.
Next rnd (RS) K8 (10), [m1 p-st, k1] 5 times, p to 5 sts before marker, [k1, m1 p-st] 5 times. Bind off all sts loosely kwise.

FINISHING
Thread beg tail of hat into tapestry needle. Weave tail around opening at top of crown. Pull tog tightly and secure end. ❖

MATERIALS

Yarn
Hand Paint Super Chunky
by Misti Alpaca Yarns,
3½oz/100g hanks, each approx
108yd/98m (alpaca/wool)
• **2 hanks in #SCH08 fox tail**

Needles
• **Size 13 (9mm) circular**
needle, 16"/40cm long or size
to obtain gauge
• **One set (4) size 13 (9mm)**
double-pointed needles (dpns)

Notions
• **Stitch marker**

MULTICOLORED TASSEL HAT
If the fabulously dyed alpaca yarn wasn't
enough, this fun-loving hat is topped off
with an adorable shaggy tassel. It's knit
top down in a simple yet sophisticated
bamboo stitch.

SIZES
Medium (Large)

FINISHED MEASUREMENTS
Circumference 19 (21)"/48 (53.5)cm

GAUGE
10 sts and 12 rnds to 4"/10cm over
bamboo st using size 13 (9mm) circular
needle.
Take time to check gauge.

STITCH GLOSSARY
inc Knit into front and back of stitch.

BAMBOO STITCH
Rnd 1 Knit.
Rnd 2 *Yo, k2, pass yo over the k-2 sts;
rep from * around.
Rep rnds 1 and 2 for bamboo st.

HAT
Crown
With dpn, cast on 12 sts, leaving a long
tail for sewing. Divide sts over 3 needles.
Join, taking care not to twist sts on
needles, pm for beg of rnds.
Rnd 1 Knit.
Rnd 2 *K1, inc in next st; rep from *
around—18 sts.
Rnd 3 and all foll odd rnds *Yo, k2, pass
yo over the k-2 sts; rep from * around.
Rnd 4 *K2, inc in next st; rep from *
around—24 sts.

Rnd 6 *K3, inc in next st; rep from *
around—30 sts.
Rnd 8 *K4, inc in next st; rep from *
around—36 sts.
Rnd 10 *K5, inc in next st; rep from *
around—42 sts.
Rnd 12 *K6, inc in next st; rep from *
around—48 sts.
For Large size only
Rnd 13 *Yo, k2, pass yo over the k-2 sts;
rep from * around.
Rnd 14 *K7, inc in next st; rep from *
around—54 sts.
For both sizes
Change to circular needle.
Rise
Rnd 1 Knit.
Rnd 2 *Yo, k2, pass yo over the k-2 sts;
rep from * around. Rep rnds 1 and 2
until piece measures 8"/20.5cm from
center top of crown.
Next rnd Knit.
Next 2 rnds *K1, p1; rep from * around.
Bind off loosely in k1, p1 rib.

FINISHING
Thread beg tail into tapestry needle.
Weave tail around opening at top of
crown. Pull tog tightly and secure end.
Tassel
Cut a 13"/33cm strand of yarn; set
aside. Wrap rem yarn 64 times around a
6½"/16.5cm piece of carboard. At one end
of cardboard, wrap reserved yarn twice
around wrapped strands, then tie firmly
in a square knot. Cut wrapped strands at
opposite end to free from cardboard.
Sew tassel to top of crown using ends of
reserved yarn. ❖

jaunty

MATERIALS

Yarn
Lamb's Pride Bulky **by Brown Sheep Company**, 4oz/113g skeins, each approx 125yd/114m (wool/mohair)
• **1 skein each in #M28 chianti (A) and #M34 victorian pink (B)**

Needles
• **Size 8 and 10½ (5 and 6.5mm) circular needles, 16"/40cm long** or size to obtain gauge
• **One set (4) size 10½ (6.5mm) double-pointed needles (dpns)**

Notions
• **Stitch marker**

TWO-TONED RIBBED HAT

Famed Bloomsbury Group artist Vanessa Bell would have grabbed her needles to knit up this pretty little number. The two-toned pattern is quick and simple—it just *looks* like you worked on it for days.

SIZES
Medium (Large)

FINISHED MEASUREMENTS
Circumference 20½ (21¾)"/52 (55)cm

GAUGE
14 sts and 20 rnds to 4"/10cm over St st using size 10½ (6.5mm) circular needle. **Take time to check gauge.**

NOTES
1) When changing colors, pick up new color from under dropped color to prevent holes.
2) Carry color not in use loosely across WS of work.

STITCH GLOSSARY
inc Knit into front and back of stitch.

SLIP STITCH PATTERN
(multiple of 4 sts)
Rnds 1–3 With A, *k3, sl 1; rep from * around.
Rnd 4 With A, knit.
Rnds 5–7 With B, *k3, sl 1; rep from * around.
Rnd 8 With B, knit.
Rep rnds 1–8 for slip st pat.

TWO-COLOR RIB
(multiple of 2 sts)
Rnd 1 *With B, k1, with A, p1; rep from * around.
Rep rnd 1 for two-color rib.

HAT

Crown
With dpn and A, cast on 12 sts, leaving a long tail for sewing. Divide sts over 3 needles. Join, taking care not to twist sts on needles, pm for beg of rnds.
Rnd 1 Knit.
Rnd 2 *Inc in next st; rep from * around—24 sts.
Rnds 3–5 Knit.
Note Change to larger circular needle when there are too many sts to work comfortably on dpns.
Rnd 6 Rep rnd 2—48 sts.
Rnds 7–10 Knit.
Rnd 11 *K3, inc in next st; rep from * around—60 sts.
Rnds 12–16 Knit.
Rnd 17 *K4, inc in next st; rep from * around—72 sts.
Rnds 18–20 Knit.
For size Large only—Rnd 21 *K8, inc in next st; rep from * around—80 sts.
Rnd 22 Knit.
For both sizes—Turn-of-crown
Purl 3 rnds.
Rise
With B, knit next rnd. Rep rnds 1–8 of slip st pat 4 times.
Brim
Turn hat WS (purl side) out. Change to smaller circular needle.
Rnd 1 [K2, inc in next st] 24 (26) times, k0 (2)—96 (106) sts. Work in two-color rib for 4 rnds. Bind off loosely in rib and color pat.

FINISHING
Thread beg tail of hat into tapestry needle. Weave tail around opening at top of crown. Pull tog tightly and secure end. Fold brim over to RS. ❖

MATERIALS

Yarn
Lamb's Pride Bulky **by Brown Sheep Company**, 4oz/113g skeins, each approx 125yd/114m (wool/mohair)
- 2 (3) skeins each in #M10 creme

Needles
- Size 10½ (6.5mm) circular needle, 16"/40cm long or size to obtain gauge
- Three size 10½ (6.5mm) double-pointed needles (dpns) for 3-needle bind-off

Notions
- Stitch marker

TASSELED SKI CAP

Keep your cool while staying toasty warm. Although sure to be a snow bunny's delight, this hat is actually quite Zen-inspired. It's knit in linen stitch, which, although easy, does take time to create the flattened weave texture. It's then folded origami-like in the back before the tassels are applied, a subtle cross between East and West.

SIZES
Medium (Large)

FINISHED MEASUREMENTS
Circumference 19½ (22)"/49.5 (56)cm

GAUGE
16 sts and 28 rnds to 4"/10cm over linen st using size 10½ (6.5mm) circular needle.
Take time to check gauge.

STITCH GLOSSARY
3-needle bind-off
1) With WS tog, hold piece on two parallel dpns. Insert 3rd dpn knitwise into first st of each needle and wrap yarn around each dpn as if to knit.
2) Knit these 2 sts tog and sl them off the needles. *K the next 2 sts tog in the same manner.
3) Sl first st on 3rd dpn over the 2nd st and off the dpn. Rep from * in step 2 across row until all sts are bound off.

LINEN STITCH
(multiple of 2 sts)
Rnd 1 *K1, wyif, sl 1; rep from * around.
Rnd 2 Knit.
Rnd 3 *Wyif, sl 1, k1; rep from * around.
Rnd 4 Knit.
Rep rnds 1–4 for linen st.

HAT
Brim
With circular needle, cast on 78 (88) sts. Join, taking care not to twist sts on needle, pm for beg of rnds. Work around in linen st for 4"/10cm. Turn piece WS out.
Rise
Cont in linen st until piece measures 17"/43cm from beg (including brim). Place first 39 (44) sts on one dpn and rem 39 (44) sts on a 2nd dpn. Cont to work 3-needle bind-off.

FINISHING
Fold brim 4"/10cm over to RS. Fold hat flat. Fold right and left top corners of hat over so they meet in the center of the top edge. Tack corners together. Fold top of hat over in the opposite direction so top edge is 1"/2.5cm from top edge of brim and folds at top of hat are facing out. Tack center top edge to side of hat to secure in place.
Tassels (make 2)
Wrap yarn 28 times around a 3½"/9cm square of cardboard. Cut two 12"/30.5cm strands of yarn. Insert one strand under wrapped strands. Bring strand up to top of carboard. Even up ends, then tie in a firm square knot. Cut wrapped strands at opposite end to free tassel from cardboard. Wrap other strand 6 times around tassel, ¾"/2cm from top. Tie ends in a firm square knot. Thread ends into tapestry needle, then insert needle down through center of tassel, so needle exits at bottom. Trim tassel to even ends. Using yarn ends at top of tassel, sew tassel to right corner where corners were tacked together at top of hat. Make another tassel and sew to left corner where corners were tacked together at top of hat. ❖

Collected

MATERIALS

Yarn
Pure Wool DK **by Rowan/
Westminster Fibers, Inc.,**
1¾oz/50g balls, each approx
126yd/115m (superwash wool)
• 2 balls in #19 avocado

Needles
• **Size 6 (4mm) circular needle,
24"/61cm long** or size to
obtain gauge
• **Size 5 (3.75mm) circular needle,
16"/40cm long**
• **One set (4) size 6 (4mm)
double-pointed needles (dpns)**

Notions
• **Stitch marker**

BOBBLED TAM

You don't let anyone or anything stand
between you and great fashion. This oh-
so-chic bobbled cap, inspired by a spiky
sea anemone, is a striking accessory for
any season. Cast on starting at the brim,
then work the combination of bobbles
and vine lace upwards.

SIZES
Medium (Large)

FINISHED MEASUREMENTS
Circumference 20 (22)"/51 (56)cm

GAUGE
22 sts and 28 rnds to 4"/10cm over pat st
using larger circular needle.
Take time to check gauge.

STITCH GLOSSARY
inc Knit into front and back of stitch.
Make Bobble (MB) [K1, p1] 3 times in same
st pulling up a long lp for each st, making
6 sts from one; then pass the 5th, 4th,
3rd, 2nd and first sts over the last st made.

TWISTED RIB
(over an even number of sts)
Rnd 1 *K1 tbl, p1; rep from * around.
Rep this rnd for twisted rib.

PATTERN STITCH
(multiple of 11 sts)
Rnd 1 *MB, k10; rep from * around.
Rnd 2 *K3, k2tog, yo, k2tog leaving sts
on LH needle, k first st again then drop
both sts from LH needle, yo, SKP, k2; rep
from * around.

Rnd 3 Knit.
Rnd 4 *K2, k2tog, yo, k4, yo, SKP, k1;
rep from * around.
Rnd 5 Knit.
Rnd 6 *MB, k2tog, yo, k1, k2tog, yo
twice, SKP, k1, yo, SKP; rep from *
around.
Rnd 7 *K5, p1, k5; rep from * around.
Rnd 8 *K3, yo, SKP, k2, k2tog, yo, k2;
rep from * around.
Rnd 9 Knit.
Rnd 10 *K4, yo, SKP, k2tog, yo, k3; rep
from * around.
Rep rnds 1–10 for pat st.

HAT
With smaller circular needle, cast on 88
(96) sts. Join, taking care not to twist sts
on needle, pm for beg of rnds. Work in
twisted rib for 7 (9) rnds.
Next (inc) rnd K 0 (2), *k1, inc in next
st; rep from * around—132 (143) sts.
Change to larger circular needle. Cont in
pat st, rep rnds 1–10 5 times, then rnd 1
once. Knit next 0 (3) rnds.

Crown
Change to dpns, dividing sts evenly over
3 needles.
Next rnd *K2tog; rep from * around,
end k 0 (1)—66 (71) sts.
Next rnd Rep last rnd—33 (36) sts.
Next rnd *K2tog; rep from * around,
end k 1 (0)—17 (18) sts.
Next rnd Rep last rnd—9 sts. Cut yarn
leaving a 6"/15.5cm tail. Thread tail into
tapestry needle, then thread through rem
sts. Pull tog tightly and secure end. ❖

determined

Instructions

Humble (Continued from page 20.)

Brim
Change to dpns. Work around in k1, p1 rib for 7 rnds.

Next rnd Bind off 12 (15) sts in rib, work next 10 sts in rib, place 11 sts on RH needle on a holder, bind off next 38 (44) sts in rib, work next 10 sts in rib, place 11 sts on RH needle on a holder, bind off rem sts.

FINISHING
Thread beg tail into tapestry needle. Weave tail around opening at top of crown. Pull tog tightly and secure end.

Ties
Place 11 sts from one holder onto a smaller dpn. Join yarn. Working back and forth using 2 dpns, cont in rib pat as established for 20"/51cm. Bind off loosely in rib. Rep for second tie.❖

Fanciful (Continued from page 26.)

low water level. Also add a pair of jeans for abrasion and balanced agitation. Add 1 tablespoon dishwashing detergent and ¼ cup baking soda at beginning of wash cycle. Repeat the cycle, if necessary, until pieces are fully felted. Block pieces flat. Let air-dry.

Flower appliqués
Using pencil compass, draw a 3¾"/9.5cm diameter circle onto paper. Cut out for pattern. For each flower, pin pattern to felted piece. Cut out using sharp scissors. Cut eight 1"/2.5cm-deep notches around circle to create petals. Position flower on an earflap so bottom edge of flower is ¼"/.5cm from bottom edge of ear flap and is centered side to side. Using a single strand of D in tapestry needle, secure flower in place and embellish center with French knots (see page 96). ❖

Energetic (Continued from page 44.)

pm on LH needle.

Rnd 4 Work in rib across 33 sts; turn, pm on LH needle.

Rnd 5 Work in rib across 30 sts; turn.

Rnd 6 Work in rib across 27 sts; turn.

Rnd 7 Work in rib across 24 sts; turn.

Rnd 8 Work in rib across 21 sts; turn.

Rnd 9 Work in rib acriss 18 sts; turn.

Rnd 10 Work in rib across 15 sts; turn.

Rnd 11 Work in rib to beg of rnd marker, dropping 2 other markers.

Rnd 12 Knit. Bind off all sts loosely knitwise.

FINISHING
Thread beg tail of hat in tapestry needle. Weave tail around opening at top of crown. Pull tog tightly and secure end. Fold brim over to RS and tack in place.❖

Lively (Continued from page 46.)

(Continued from page 46.)

Beg chart VI
Rnd 1 Work 8-st pat rep 9 times. Cont to foll chart in this manner through rnd 5. Cont with A as foll:
Next rnd Knit.
Next (inc) rnd *K8, inc in next st; rep from * around—80 sts.
Next rnd Knit.
Beg chart VII
Rnd 1 Work 20-st pat rep 4 times. Cont to foll chart in this manner through rnd 5. Cont with A as foll:
Next rnd Knit. Change to circular needle.
Next (inc) rnd *K4, inc in next st; rep from * around—96 sts.
Next rnd Knit.
Rise
Beg chart VIII
Rnd 1 Work 8-st pat rep 12 times. Cont to foll chart in this manner through rnd 6. Cont with A as foll:
Next rnd Knit.
Next (inc) rnd *K7, inc in next st; rep from * around—108 sts.
Next rnd Knit.
Beg chart IX
Rnd 1 Work 4-st pat rep 27 times. Cont to foll chart in this manner through rnd 3. Cont with A as foll:
Next rnd Knit.
For Medium size only
Next rnd Knit.
For Large size only
Next (inc) rnd [K12, inc in next st] 8 times, k4—116 sts.

For both sizes
Next rnd Knit.
Beg chart X
Rnd 1 Work 4-st pat rep 27 (29) times. Cont to foll chart in this manner through rnd 4. Cont with A as foll:
Next 3 rnds Knit.
Beg chart XI
Rnd 1 Work 4-st pat rep 27 (29) times. Cont to foll chart in this manner through rnd 3. Cont with A as foll:
Next 3 rnds Knit.
Brim and earflaps
Change to F. Work around in k2, p2 rib for 2"/5cm.
Next rnd Work in rib across first 38 (41) sts, bind off next 32 (34) sts, work in rib to end. Working back and forth, using two circular needles, cont in rib pat for 2"/5cm. Bind off loosely in rib pat.

FINISHING
Thread beg tail of hat into tapestry needle. Weave tail around opening at top of crown. Pull tog tightly and secure end.
Pompom
Make a 3"/7.5cm diameter pompom using B, D and E (see page 96). Sew to top of hat.❖

Color Key
- Chambray (A)
- Rose Spice (B)
- Yucca Mix (C)
- Chianti (D)
- Cardinal (E)
- Blue Violet (F)
- Turquoise Mix (G)

Chart I

Chart II

Chart III

Chart IV

Chart V

Chart VI
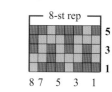

Chart VII
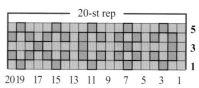

Chart VIII
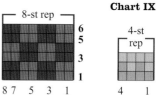

Chart IX

Chart X
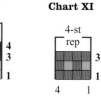

Chart XI

Instructions

Noble (Continued from page 60.)

p4, m1, k1, sl marker, k1, m1, p to 1 st before marker, m1, k1—61 sts.

Rnd 20 K2, p5, k7, p1, inc in next st, p1, k1, p1, inc in next st, p1, k7, p5, k2, sl marker, k2, p to 2 sts before next marker, k2—63 sts.

Rnd 21 K1, m1, p4, p2tog, k3, yo, k1, yo, [k3, p3] twice, k3, yo, k1, yo, k3, p2tog, p4, m1, k1, sl marker, k1, m1, p to 1 st before marker, m1, k1—69 sts.

Rnd 22 K2, p5, k9, p1, inc in next st, p1, k3, p1, inc in next st, p1, k9, p5, k2, sl marker, k2, p to 2 sts before next marker, k2—71 sts.

Rnd 23 K1, m1, p4, p2tog, k4, yo, k1, yo, k4, p4, k3, p4, k4, yo, k1, yo, k4 p2tog, p4, M1, k1, sl marker, k1, m1, p to 1 st before marker, m1, k1—77 sts.

Rnd 24 K2, p5, k11, p1, inc in next st, p2, k3, p2, inc in next st, p1, k11, p5, k2 sl marker, k2, p to 2 sts before next marker, k2—79 sts.

Rnd 25 K1, M1, p4, p2tog, k2tog, k7, k2tog, p5, k3, p5, k2tog, k7, k2tog, p2tog, p4, M1, k1, sl marker, k1, M1, p to 1 st before marker, M1, k1—77 sts.

Rnd 26 K2, p5, k9, p5, inc in next st, k1, inc in next st, p5, k9, p5, k2, sl marker, k2, p to 2 sts before next marker, k2—79 sts.

Working straight

Note St count will inc and dec from rnd to rnd.

Rnd 27 K2, p3, p2tog, k2tog, k5, k2tog, p5, [yo, p1] twice, k1, [p1, yo] twice, p5, k2tog, k5, k2tog, p2tog, p3, k2, sl marker, k2, p to 2 sts before next marker, k2.

Rnd 28 K2, p4, k7, p5, k3, inc in next st, k1, inc in next st, k3, p5, k7, p4, k2, sl marker, k2, p to 2 sts before next marker, k2.

Rnd 29 K2, p2, p2tog, k2tog, k3, k2tog, p5, [k1, yo] twice, [k1, p2] twice, k1, [yo, k1] twice, p5, k2tog, k3, k2tog, p2tog, p2, k2, sl marker, k2, p to 2 sts before next marker, k2.

Rnd 30 K2, p3, k5, p5, k5, p1, inc in next st, k1, inc in next st, p1, k5, p5, k5, p3, k2, sl marker, k2, p to 2 sts before next marker, k2.

Rnd 31 K2, p1, p2tog, k2tog, k1, k2tog, p5, k2, yo, k1, yo, k2, p3, k1, p3, k2, yo, k1, yo, k2, p5, k2tog, k1, k2tog, p2tog, p1, k2, sl marker, k2, p to 2 sts before next marker, k2.

Rnd 32 K2, p2, k3, p5, k7, p1, inc in next st, p1, k1, p1, inc in next st, p1, k7, p5, k3, p2, k2, sl marker, k2, p to 2 sts before next marker, k2.

Rnd 33 K2, p2tog, k3tog, p5, k3, yo, k1, yo, [k3, p3] twice, k3, yo, k1, yo, k3, p5, k3tog, p2tog, k2, sl marker, k2, p to 2 sts before next marker, k2.

Rnd 34 K2, p7, k9, p1, inc in next st, p1, k3, p1, inc in next st, p1, k9, p7, k2, sl marker, k2, p to 2 sts before next marker, k2.

Rnd 35 K2, p5, p2tog, k4, yo, k1, yo, k4, p4, k3, p4, k4, yo, k1, yo, k4, p2tog, p5, k2, sl marker, k2, p to 2 sts before next marker, k2.

Rnd 36 K2, p6, k11, p1, inc in next st, p2, k3, p2, inc in next st, p1, k11, p6, k2, sl marker, k2, p to 2 sts before next marker, k2.

Rnd 37 K2, p4, p2tog, k2tog, k7, k2tog, p5, k3, p5, k2tog, k7, k2tog, p2tog, p4, k2, sl marker, k2, p to 2 sts before next marker, k2.

Rnd 38 K2, p5, k9, p5, inc in next st, k1, inc in next st, p5, k9, p5, k2, sl marker, k2, p to 2 sts before next marker, k2.

Rnd 39 K2, p3, p2tog, k2tog, k5, k2tog, p5, [yo, p1] twice, k1, [p1, yo] twice, p5, k2tog, k5, k2tog, p2tog, p3, k2, sl marker, k2, p to 2 sts before next marker, k2.

Rnd 40 K2, p4, k7, p5, k3, inc in next st, k1, inc in next st, k3, p5, k7, p4, k2, sl marker, k2, p to 2 sts before next marker, k2.

Rnd 41 K2, p2, p2tog, k2tog, k3, k2tog, p5, [k1, yo] twice, [k1, p2] twice, k1, [yo, k1] twice, p5, k2tog, k3, k2tog, p2tog, p2,

k2, sl marker, k2, p to 2 sts before next marker, k2.

Rnd 42 K2, p3, k5, p5, k5, p1, inc in next st, k1, inc in next st, p1, k5, p5, k5, p3, k2, sl marker, k2, p to 2 sts before next marker, k2.

Rnd 43 K2, p1, p2tog, k2tog, k1, k2tog, p5, k2, yo, k1, yo, k2, p3, k1, p3, k2, yo, k1, yo, k2, p5, k2tog, k1, k2tog, p2tog, p1, k2, sl marker, k2, p to 2 sts before next marker, k2.

Rnd 44 K2, p2, k3, p5, k7, p1, inc in next st, p1, k1, p1, inc in next st, p1, k7, p5, k3, p2, k2, sl marker, k2, p to 2 sts before next marker, k2.

Rnd 45 K2, p2tog, k3tog, p5, k3, yo, k1, yo, [k3, p3] twice, k3, yo, k1, yo, k3, p5, k3tog, p2tog, k2, sl marker, k2, p to 2 sts before next marker, k2.

Rnd 46 K2, p7, k9, p1, inc in next st, p1, k3, p1, inc in next st, p1, k9, p7, k2, sl marker, k2, p to 2 sts before next marker, k2.

Rep rnds 35–46, 7 times more, then rnds 35 and 36 once—83 sts.

Side shaping

Rnd 1 K2, p2tog, p2, p2tog, k2tog, k7, k2tog, p6, yo, k1, yo, p6, k2tog, k7, k2tog, p2tog, p2, p2tog, k2, sl marker, k2, p2tog, p to 4 sts before marker, p2tog, k2—75 sts.

Rnd 2 K2, p4, k9, p6, k3, p6, k9, p4, k2, sl marker, k2, p to 2 sts before next marker, k2.

Rnd 3 K2, p2tog, p2, k2tog, k5, k2tog, p6, [k1, yo] twice, k1, p6, k2tog, k5, k2tog, p2, p2tog, k2, sl marker, k2, p2tog, p to 4 sts before marker, p2tog, k2—69 sts.

Rnd 4 K2, p3, k7, p6, k5, p6, k7, p3, k2, sl marker, k2, p to 2 sts before next marker, k2.

Rnd 5 K2, p2tog, p1, k2tog, k3, k2tog, p6, k2, yo, k1, yo, k2, p6, k2tog, k3, k2tog, p1, p2tog, k2, sl marker, k2, p2tog, p to 4 sts before marker, p2tog, k2—63 sts.

Rnd 6 K2, p2, k5, p6, k7, p6, k5, p2, k2, sl marker, k2, p to 2 sts before next marker, k2.

Rnd 7 K2, p2tog, k2tog, k1, k2tog, p6, k3, yo, k1, yo, k3, p6, k2tog, k1, k2tog, p2tog, k2, sl marker, k2, p2tog, p to 4 sts before marker, p2tog, k2—57 sts.

Rnd 8 K2, p1, k3, p6, k9, p6, k3, p1, k2, sl marker, k2, p to 2 sts before next marker, k2.

Rnd 9 K2, p1, k3tog, p2tog, p4, k4, yo, k1, yo, k4, p4, p2tog, k3tog, p1, k2, sl marker, k2, p2tog, p to 4 sts before marker, p2tog, k2—51 sts.

Rnd 10 K2, p7, k11, p7, k2, sl marker, k2, p to 2 sts before next marker, k2.

Rnd 11 K2, p2tog, p5, k2tog, k7, k2tog, p5, p2tog, k2, sl marker, k2, p2tog, p to 4 sts before marker, p2tog, k2—45 sts.

Rnd 12 K2, p6, k9, p6, k2, sl marker, k2, p to 2 sts before next marker, k2.

Rnd 13 K2, p2tog, p4, k2tog, k5, k2tog, p4, p2tog, k2, sl marker, k2, p2tog, p to 4 sts before marker, p2tog, k2—39 sts.

Rnd 14 K2, p5, k7, p5, k2, sl marker, k2, p to 2 sts before next marker, k2.

Rnd 15 K2, p2tog, p3, k2tog, k3, k2tog, p3, p2tog, k2, sl marker, k2, p2tog, p to 4 sts before marker, p2tog, k2—33 sts.

Rnd 16 K2, p4, k5, p4, k2, sl marker, k2, p to 2 sts before next marker, k2.

Rnd 17 K2, p2tog, p2, k2tog, k1, k2tog, p2, p2tog, k2, sl marker, k2, p2tog, p to 4 sts before marker, p2tog, k2—27 sts.

Rnd 18 K2, p3, k3, p3, k2, sl marker, k2, p to 2 sts before next marker, k2.

Rnd 19 K2, p2tog, p1, k3tog, p1, p2tog, k2, sl marker, k2, p2tog, p to 4 sts before marker, p2tog, k2—21 sts.

Rnd 20 K2, p5, k2, sl marker, k2, p to 2 sts before next marker, k2.

Rnd 21 K2, p2tog, p1, p2tog, k2, sl marker, k2, p2tog, p to 4 sts before marker, p2tog, k2—17 sts.

Rnd 22 K2, p3, k2, sl marker, k2, p to 2 sts before next marker, k2.

Rnd 23 K2, p3tog, k2, sl marker, k2, p2tog, p to 4 sts before marker, p2tog, k2—13 sts.

Rnd 24 K2, p2tog, k2, drop 2nd marker, k to end—12 sts.

Second tie

Work around in St st for 15"/38cm. Bind off loosely knitwise.

FINISHING

Sew ends of ties closed. Using sewing needle and thread, sew a pearl to base of each pair of leaves and at base of single leaf. ✤

Idealistic (Pattern on page 78.)

Topping It All Off

FINDING YOUR PERFECT FIT

When you see hats for sale in stores, more often than not they're labeled "one size fits all" (OSFA). However, hat labels should more accurately read "one size fits most," because although the "average" adult head circumference is 20 inches, heads actually range in size from 19 to 23 inches. That's a five-inch difference from the smallest to the largest, which is not insubstantial. This means that if your head is the smallest size, it will swim in the ordinary one-size-fits-all hat, and if it is the largest size, you may feel as if you're wearing a vise on your head. The good news though is that by making your own hats, you can get a custom fit, a better fit than that provided by store-bought hats. The patterns in this book are written for two sizes—medium and large—or, for certain styles in which size is not as important, one size fits all.

Measuring for Correct Hat Size

To determine your hat size, wrap a measuring tape around your head, lining it up with the point on the forehead where most hat brims will settle—usually midway down the forehead—and the parallel point at the back of the head. Your head circumference will probably be in the 19-to-23-inch range. In a few cases, a person might have an unusually smaller head, usually a woman's at 18 inches, or an unusually larger head, often a man's head at 24 inches. Smaller measurements are usually associated with children's sizes and have not been included in this book. Check the table below to determine what size hat you should knit.

Designing a Hat to Fit

For most styles of knitted hats, you should make the hat itself smaller than your head measurement so it clings to the crown and doesn't fall down around the eyes. How much smaller should it be? Between one to two inches depending on the hat style itself. I usually adhere to a 2-inch margin. However, again, depending on a hat's style and how it should fit, I vary this as needed.

Making adjustments to a pattern is done via the yarn gauge. For instance, if your head measures 21 inches, and you want to knit a 19-inch hat, just multiply the yarn's gauge per inch by 19 to get the final brim stitch count.

Variations in Sizing Hats

Many sports styles like beanies and skull caps are meant to cling so they remain on your head in inclement weather and when you're participating in sports. But some hat styles should actually "sit" on the head. Berets and tams, for example, are usually made to be less tight so that they sit on the crown somewhat. Shaped felted hats sit rather than hug the head as well.

Another consideration in determining a finished hat size is whether the brim is to be folded up or not. Doubling a brim, be it ribbed or in any other stitch pattern, requires an allowance of a few more stitches to accommodate the width of the doubled-up fabric when worn. Therefore, even though an average head measures 20 inches, the number of stitches to be cast on (or to end with if knitting from the top down) won't necessarily reflect the usual 18 inches (20 minus 2). You'll observe this in the following collection of patterns, but have no fear. If you are achieving the stated gauge, these hat styles have been tried and tested and are sized to provide you with the best-fitting hat possible.

	Medium Size Hat	Large Size Hat
Head circumference	19–21"/48.5–53.5cm	22–23"/56–58.5cm
Average hat measurement (cling-fit beanie or skull cap; varies by hat style)	18"/46cm	21"/53.5cm

HAT ANATOMY

A typical hat is made up of a number of parts. It helps to know their names when you are making a hat, so you can follow the pattern more easily. Keep in mind that not every hat design includes all of these elements.

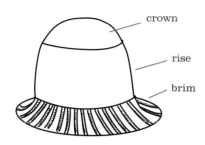

Crown The portion of a hat that covers the top of the head.

Turn-of-crown The point that delineates the crown from the rise.

Rise The upright portion of the hat that extends down from the crown.

Brim or band An optional projection from the bottom of the hat's rise made horizontally around the circumference of the hat.

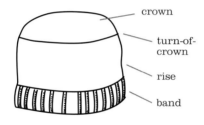

ABBREVIATIONS

approx	approximately
beg	begin(ning)
CC	contrasting color
ch	chain
cm	centimeter(s)
cn	cable needle
cont	continu(e)(ing)
dec	decreas(e)(ing)
dpn	double-pointed needle(s)
foll	follow(s)(ing)
g	gram(s)
inc	increas(e)(ing)
ITR	in the round
k	knit
LH	left-hand
lp(s)	loop(s)
m	meter(s)
MC	main color
mm	millimeter(s)
m1	make one
m1 p-st	make 1 purl stitch
oz	ounce(s)
p	purl
pat(s)	pattern(s)
pm	place marker
psso	pass slip stitch(es) over
rem	remain(s)(ing)
rep	repeat
RH	right-hand
rnd(s)	round(s)
RS	right side(s)
SKP	slip 1, knit 1, pass slip stitch over—one stitch has been decreased

SK2P	slip 1, knit 2 together, pass slip stitch over the knit 2 together—two stitches have been decreased
S2KP	slip 2 stitches together, knit 1, pass 2 slip stitches over knit 1
sl	slip
sl st	slip stitch
ssk	slip, slip, knit
sssk	slip, slip, slip, knit
st(s)	stitch(es)
St st	stockinette stitch
tbl	through back loop(s)
tog	together
WS	wrong side(s)
wyib	with yarn in back
wyif	with yarn in front
yd	yard(s)
yo	yarn over needle
*****	repeat directions following * as many times as indicated
[ ]	repeat directions inside brackets as many times as indicated

EMBROIDERY STITCHES

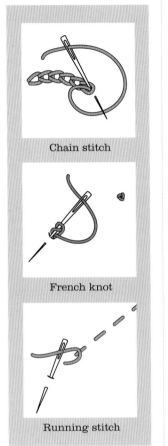

Chain stitch

French knot

Running stitch

HOW TO MAKE A POMPOM

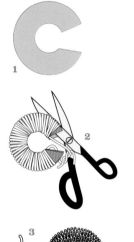

1. Take two circular pieces of cardboard the width of the desired pompom and cut a center hole. Then cut a pie-shaped wedge out of each circle.

2. Hold the two circles together and wrap the yarn tightly around the cardboard. Then carefully cut around the cardboard.

3. Tie a piece of yarn tightly between the two circles. Remove the cardboard and trim the pompom.

YARN RESOURCES

Berroco, Inc.
P.O. Box 367
14 Elmdale Road
Uxbridge, MA 01569
www.berroco.com

Blue Sky Alpacas
P.O. Box 88
Cedar, MN 55011
www.blueskyalpacas.com

Brown Sheep Company
100662 County Road 16
Mitchell, NE 69357
www.brownsheep.com

Classic Elite Yarns
122 Western Avenue
Lowell, MA 01851
www.classiceliteyarns.com

Debbie Bliss
Distributed by KFI
www.debbieblissonline.com

Filatura Di Crosa
Distributed by Tahki•Stacy Charles, Inc.

Jade Sapphire Exotic Fibres
866-857-3897
www.jadesapphire.com

KFI
P.O. Box 336
315 Bayview Avenue
Amityville, NY 11701
www.knittingfever.com

Lion Brand Yarn
34 West 15th Street
New York, NY 10011
www.lionbrand.com

Lorna's Laces
4229 N. Honore Street
Chicago, IL 60613
www.lornaslaces.net

Misti Alpaca Yarns
P.O. Box 2532
Glen Ellyn, IL 60138
www.mistialpaca.com

Nashua Handknits
Distributed by Westminster Fibers, Inc.

Ozark Handspun
P.O. Box 1405
Jefferson City, MO 65102
www.ozarkhandspun.com

Patons
320 Livingstone Avenue South
Listowel, Ontario
N4W 3H3 Canada
www.patonsyarns.com

Plymouth Yarn Co.
500 Lafayette Street
Bristol, PA 19007
www.plymouthyarn.com

Rowan
Distributed by Westminster Fibers, Inc.
UK: Green Lane Mill
Holmfirth
HD9 2DX England
www.knitrowan.com

Schulana
Distributed by Skacel Collection, Inc.

Skacel Collection, Inc.
8041 South 180th Street
Kent, WA 98032
www.skacelknitting.com

Tahki•Stacy Charles, Inc.
70-30 80th St. Building 36
Ridgewood, NY 11385
www.tahkistacycharles.com

Twinkle By Wenlan
Distributed by Classic Elite Yarns

Valley Yarns
75 Service Center Road
Northampton, MA 01060
www.yarn.com

Westminster Fibers, Inc.
165 Ledge Street
Nashua, NH 03060
www.westminsterfibers.com